Advance Praise for *Conquering the Chaos*

"India tests the capabilities of any global company to the hilt. This book tells you what it takes to crack the India code. Great reading."
— Jean-Pascal Tricoire, President and CEO, Schneider Electric

"A fascinating read on how to succeed in India and why it is relevant for winning in other emerging markets. This is a must-read for all executives interested in global growth."
— Mukesh D. Ambani, Chairman and Managing Director, Reliance Industries

"Succeeding in emerging markets is of tremendous strategic significance for every multinational company. If you are looking for practical advice on how to win—not just in India, but in all emerging markets—Ravi Venkatesan's book tells you how."
— Nandan Nilekani, Chairman, UID Authority, Government of India; former CEO, Infosys

"*Conquering the Chaos* is a practical playbook for business success in India. Ravi Venkatesan's hands-on experience and extensive research will make this your go-to book for India. Even those who are currently succeeding in India will find helpful insights here."
— Tom Linebarger, Chairman and CEO, Cummins Inc.

"A brilliant, contrarian, and very readable manual on how to succeed in India and other emerging markets."
— Anand Mahindra, Chairman and Managing Director, Mahindra and Mahindra

"Ravi Venkatesan has given us the guidebook to successful growth in India we so desperately need. He provides us with down-to-earth managerial insights that will most certainly determine the success or failure of ventures in this critical economy. A must-read for anyone interested in globalization, India, and the successful enterprise."
— Leonard Schlesinger, President, Babson College; former professor, Harvard Business School

"A brilliant book that I finished in a single sitting."
— K. V. Kamath, Chairman, Infosys Limited; Chairman, ICICI Bank

"India is an important market for global companies and will become even more important in the future. *Conquering the Chaos* tells you the basic do's and don'ts of entering and managing a successful business in India, in simple and compelling terms."

—Tim Solso, former Chairman and CEO, Cummins;
Member of the Board, General Motors

"Amazingly strong on concepts and rich in experience, Ravi Venkatesan combines deep insights with powerful practical tools for how companies can succeed in India. Anyone interested in understanding India and emerging markets must read this book."

—Srikant M. Datar, Arthur Lowes Dickinson Professor of Accounting,
Harvard Business School

"A unique combination of timeliness and clarity regarding the great opportunities and eye-watering challenges of sensibly investing and honestly doing business in India. It can be hugely rewarding, but the challenges are indeed incredible! Ravi Venkatesan describes them, and more, with clarity and rare honesty."

—Ashok Ganguly, Member of Parliament, India; former Chairman,
Hindustan Unilever

"*Conquering the Chaos* is a provocative and candid take on doing business in India. It should be on the reading list of anyone interested in globalization and emerging markets."

—Samuel R. Allen, Chairman and CEO, Deere & Company

"Ravi Venkatesan's book is the most tough, honest, unique, solutions-based, and strategic book on doing business in India. A must-read for all CEOs engaged with the economies of tomorrow."

—Tarun Das, former Director General, Confederation of Indian Industry

"Ravi Venkatesan has written an important book. It mixes real-life, insightful experience of doing business across different industries in India with a more general explanatory model. I believe it is a must-read for business leaders of global companies."

—Leif Johansson, Chairman, Ericsson and Astra-Zeneca

"This is an important and insightful book for any global company wanting to build a business in India. It has breadth, depth, and perspective, and highlights the importance of culture and values."

—Carl Henric Svanberg, Chairman, BP and Volvo

"While this book provides powerful insights into a complex country and culture, the more fundamental lessons center on transformational leadership in our twenty-first-century world."

—Ann Fudge, former Chairman and CEO, Young & Rubicam

WIN IN INDIA,
WIN EVERYWHERE

CONQUERING
THE
CHAOS

RAVI VENKATESAN

HARVARD BUSINESS REVIEW PRESS
BOSTON, MASSACHUSETTS

Copyright 2013 Harvard Business School Publishing Corporation

All rights reserved
Printed in the United States of America
10 9 8

No part of this publication may be reproduced, stored in or introduced into a retrieval system, or transmitted, in any form, or by any means (electronic, mechanical, photocopying, recording, or otherwise), without the prior permission of the publisher. Requests for permission should be directed to permissions@hbsp.harvard.edu, or mailed to Permissions, Harvard Business School Publishing, 60 Harvard Way, Boston, Massachusetts 02163.

The web addresses referenced in this book were live and correct at the time of the book's publication but may be subject to change.

Library of Congress Cataloging-in-Publication Data

Venkatesan, Ravi.
  Conquering the chaos : win in India, win everywhere / Ravi Venkatesan.
    pages cm
  ISBN 978-1-4221-8430-1
  1. International business enterprises—India. 2. Business enterprises, Foreign—India. 3. Corporate culture—India. 4. Joint ventures—India. I. Title.
  HD2899.V38 2013
  658'.0490954—dc23
                          2012051720

ISBN13: 978-1-4221-8430-1
eISBN: 978-1-4221-8431-8

The paper used in this publication meets the requirements of the American National Standard for Permanence of Paper for Publications and Documents in Libraries and Archives Z39.48-1992.

Dedicated to honest and upright

government officials in all emerging markets

for the courage they show every day

CONTENTS

1

India

A DEFINING CHOICE

India should be viewed less as a difficult market where
strange things are happening, and more as a market that is simply
ahead of many other markets in its evolution ... If we don't figure out
how to win in India, we could end up losing in a lot
of other geographies around the world. Conversely, if we
can win in India, we can win everywhere.

—STEPHEN ELOP, CEO, NOKIA

Why have only a handful of multinational companies succeeded in India, while so many simply muddle along? What does success in India look like and what does it take to win in India? With India recently losing much of her shine, is that even important? Why should multinational companies bother with India's chaos?

My interest in trying to understand whether India actually matters to most multinational corporations stems from my experience over the past fifteen years in helping to build two billion-dollar businesses for American companies in India, first for engine maker Cummins Inc. and later for software giant Microsoft Inc. Both have been successful in India. Cummins India has built a dominant 60-plus percent market share in both the diesel engines and the diesel generating sets businesses (estimated at over 50 percent market share). It is a highly respected company. Similarly, Microsoft India is far and away the leader in the software business in India and consistently ranks among the best employers and most admired brands in India.

There's one difference, though.

India contributes roughly 10 percent of Cummins's global revenues and even more of its profits and growth, but Microsoft derives just 1.5 percent of its global revenues from India. More importantly, if you extrapolate their growth rates for the next ten years, the situation won't change much. If Microsoft grows its global revenues by a conservative 7 percent to 10 percent over the decade, and its India business expands at, say, 20 percent or 25 percent compound annual growth rate (CAGR), by 2022, India would still account for only about 5 percent of the company's revenues. Its contribution to Microsoft's global growth would also remain modest. Thus, India matters deeply to Cummins, but not as much to Microsoft.

Microsoft is hardly unique. Many other well-run companies such as Caterpillar, Toyota, and Daimler face the same situation. In fact, most multinational companies see India primarily as a talent pool for offshoring knowledge and a market that will be important someday down the road. As a result, India typically accounts for a trivial 1 percent or less of their global revenues and profits, and an anemic 5 percent or so of their global growth. The Indian market's numbers for these companies are akin to a rounding-off error, and given their trajectories, they will still be irrelevantly small a decade from now. Would that not have strategic consequences?

These numbers and their potential consequences bothered me.

This prompted me to spend a year interviewing the CEOs and senior leaders of around thirty companies in different industries. I also convened meetings of some of the most accomplished country managers in India, including the leaders of Nokia, GE, Dell, Honeywell, Volvo, Schneider

Electric, JCB, Bosch, Unilever, and Nestlé. I tested our hypotheses with some of the global leaders to whom they report such as Honeywell's Shane Tedjarati, Walmart Asia's Scott Price, Ericsson CEO Hans Vestberg, and Standard Chartered Bank's executive director, Jaspal Bindra.

My research and interviews led me to uncover some fundamental issues that I will tackle in this book.[1] I will be addressing questions such as, How should senior leaders of multinational companies think about India and other emerging markets? Why is "winning in India" so hard? Why have some companies succeeded spectacularly in the same challenging environment? What are the likely consequences of failing to build a strong market position in India? My focus throughout will be on providing practical perspectives, real-world anecdotes, and actionable takeaways for operating managers.

Should India Matter?

India appears to be at a tipping point. Global success in information technology, a decade of growth, and some excellent public relations enabled the country to change people's perception of it. After decades of being equated with Pakistan, India has increasingly come to be associated with China in terms of potential. However, the past couple of years have been devastating. Massive corruption scandals, weak kleptocratic political leadership, divisive politics, stalled reforms, and a decelerating economy are making Indians and foreigners alike question the future. Gone is the hubris that dared India to think it could do better than China or even some developed countries.

THE PLUSES. That said, India does have many things going for it. One is the large pool of talent. It may be getting harder and costlier to find and keep good talent, but India remains one of the most important places in the world to do knowledge work, ranging from managing business processes to running information technology systems, and for engineering work ranging from drafting and testing to sophisticated design and analysis. Shifting those processes to India has the ability to change companies' cost structures and add several hundred basis points to their profitability. Some, such as IBM (142,000 employees in India as of 2012), Honeywell (20,000), and Dell (28,000), have leveraged this effectively, but others, particularly European and Japanese companies, have yet to harness the IQ and energy of young Indians. (Offshoring and outsourcing are well covered elsewhere, and I will not spend much time on them; my focus in this book is the Indian market.)

The second plus is the intrinsic strength of the economy. It is difficult to ignore the progress that India has made over the past three decades, albeit in fits and starts. In his book, *India Grows at Night*, Gurucharan Das says that "India grows at night … when the government sleeps," suggesting that the country has done well despite, not because of, the state. India is a story of private success trumping public failure. Figure 1-1, a graph of India's GDP growth from 1980 to 2010, illustrates this quite dramatically; what's impressive is the country's sustained economic growth despite many different governments in power, some more effective than others (see figure 1-1).

Several reasons account for these economic gains, such as the ambitions and drive of India's youthful population—the so-called demographic dividend. A healthy savings rate as well as rising rural incomes driven by pricing support for crops, significant improvements in literacy and education, a culture of entrepreneurship and improvisation (although not quite innovation as it is commonly understood), a competent managerial class, a reasonably sound banking system and capital market, and a fair and activist Supreme Court have contributed as well.

Moreover, India has become more federal, with power shifting to the state governments from the central government. Growth is increasingly powered by the states rather than by policy decisions in Delhi, and the states' economic performance, even that of perennially

FIGURE 1-1

Growth of India's GDP

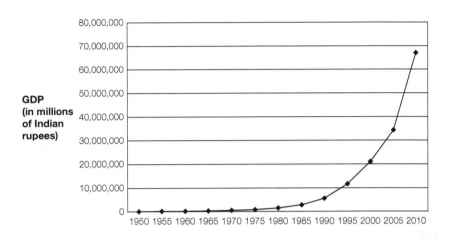

backward Bihar, has been encouraging. Above all, there has been an irreversible awakening of the aspirations of a billion people. The growth genie is out of the bottle, and India is on an irreversible course of development.

Mukesh Ambani, India's richest businessman, puts it well: "India is a bottom-up not a top-down story." No country except China has the same medium- and long-term economic potential as India. Even in a scenario of modest 6 percent to 7 percent GDP growth, by 2030, the country will have the largest middle-class population and share of middle-class consumption in the world. India's progress has prompted frequent comparison with the aerodynamically challenged bumble-bee, which theoretically should be incapable of flight. Yet, both continue to defy the odds.[2]

THE MINUSES. Nearly fifty years ago, John Kenneth Galbraith, the US ambassador to India and an ardent Indophile, called India "a functioning anarchy." In that one respect, not much has changed.

Negating the considerable intrinsic strengths of India is corrupt and incompetent governance at all levels of the nation: central, state, city, and village. Nearly 25 percent of the members of India's lower house of Parliament have had criminal cases filed against them, ranging from kidnapping and murder to extortion and robbery. Unbounded greed and corruption have resulted in politicians, bureaucrats, and businesspeople becoming predatory to an extent seen only in some African dictatorships and the post–Soviet Union era in Russia. Well-connected industrialists, politicians, and public officials have conspired to carve up India's natural resources, ranging from mineral resources to land and the telecom spectrum.

However, the system of patronage and crony capitalism has been paralyzed, as its workings stand exposed by a mixture of fearless activists, Supreme Court interventions, government audits, a feisty media, and the public itself, angry over graft and drift. Scarcely a month goes by without the exposure of yet another scandal, such as the 2G telecom scandal in 2010, which *Time* dubbed the second-biggest scandal after Watergate.[3] Other scandals have since come to light in the power and mining sectors, as well as several land deals.[4]

Corruption in India isn't limited to crony capitalism. Graft has permeated the fabric of Indian society, and at every step, officials harass individuals and companies, whether it is to register a land transaction, renew a multitude of licenses, clear a shipment through customs, or win a public tender. Companies find themselves continuously extorted by inspectors who handle pollution control, labor laws, and indirect taxes, and they must comply with arcane regulations dating back a century or more. Their choice is between spending countless hours defending themselves or paying one more tax to individuals so they can focus on business.

The ineptness of the government in driving essential policy reforms has also become legendary. Maimed by arrogance and corruption scandals, a coalition government, led by the Congress

Party, has struggled in recent times to pass unpopular measures because of opposition from coalition partners and political rivals. For example, the government tried to open up the retail sector to foreign investment in 2011, only to reverse itself because of the opposition of its political allies. In December 2012, a frustrated but determined prime minister finally used all his political capital to push the measure through Parliament, but left the final decision to each state. Global retailers must negotiate licenses with each state they wish to enter.

Acquiring land remains tricky, and obtaining environmental clearances can take years. According to G. V. K. Reddy, whose company was responsible for the recent overhaul of Mumbai's airport, the developer had to deal with over 220 cases over property, environmental, and labor disputes in the process. Creating a one-stop shop for project approvals and unifying regulations across state borders would smooth the road for developers. However, India's land acquisition law has not been modified since 1894, and Parliament has held up a new law for months, as lawmakers struggle to find the middle ground between industrial development and defending the rights of small landowners.

For these and other reasons, critical infrastructure projects have been delayed. Despite the government's ambitious aims of attracting $1 trillion in infrastructure investments, India is littered with stalled projects while Indians endure pothole-filled and garbage-laden roads, congested ports and airports, creaky railways, overflowing drains, and the absence of clean drinking water. Power plants stand idle, crippled by shortages of fuel, while 600 million Indians were stranded without power for two days in July 2012 and the citizens of the southern state of Tamil Nadu endure daily power outages lasting twelve hours or more. The list of woes when it comes to infrastructure is endless.

A final issue, one that has become a Frankenstein monster, is taxation. Not only is the tax regime complex and deliberately ambiguous, but to fund the massive fiscal deficit caused by unsustainable welfare programs, the revenue authorities have collection targets. They have unprecedented discretionary powers, which they wield like a blunt weapon. All companies face harassment, but multinational companies make particularly easy targets, as companies like Vodafone, HP, Shell, Nokia, Microsoft, and Nestlé will attest. The most dramatic example is the bruising dispute between the finance ministry and Vodafone, India's largest foreign investor, over a disputed $2 billion capital gains tax bill. To get around a Supreme Court ruling in Vodafone's favor, the finance ministry wanted to amend the law retroactively to April 1962! Whatever the final outcome, the incident has dented India's image in the eyes of investors everywhere, while raising serious concerns among business leaders and governments. A key economic adviser to the prime minister comments: "A government that changes the law retrospectively at will to fit its interpretation introduces tremendous uncertainty into business decisions, and it sets itself outside the law. India has missed an excellent opportunity to show its respect for the rule of law even if it believes the law is poorly written. That is far more damaging than any tax revenues it could obtain by being capricious."[5]

The Vodafone case, the harassment of respected companies and professionals, and the proposed General Anti-Avoidance Rules (GAAR), an ambiguous attempt to prevent tax evasion, are creating uncertainty, anger, and anxiety at a time when the government desperately needs to attract more foreign investment. One CEO of a multinational, who asked not to be named, says the unpredictability of the tax regime puts India at par with the Democratic Republic of the Congo, adding that it is contradictory when the Indian government says it needs foreign investments but creates investor-unfriendly policies at the same time.

All these factors have together made India one of the most challenging countries in which to operate. Ratan Tata, the chairperson of the Tata Group, cautioned that if the government didn't step in and uphold the rule of law, "there was every possibility that India could become a banana republic."[6] Sunil Mittal, the highly influential and cautious chairperson of telecom operator Bharti Airtel, didn't mince his words either: "This has been the most destructive period of regulatory environment I have seen in 16 years," he publicly stated in May 2012.[7]

The numbers bear him out. According to the World Bank, India ranks 133 of 183 countries in terms of ease of doing business (falling from 120 in 2007), 169 in terms of taxation, and, despite the public outrage against corruption, matters may be getting worse as India sank 11 places to number 95 in 2011. The Indian economy has slowed to a new Hindu rate of growth of 5 percent compared with the earlier 3 percent.[8]

Given the realities of dynastic rule and coalition politics, confidence in the government's abilities to tackle the enormous challenges is low. Ramachandra Guha, a historian and writer on Indian affairs, argues that instability may be India's destiny. He says that bad politics, corrupt leaders, and weak and politicized institutions mean that instability and policy incoherence may be a long-term feature.[9]

Indian companies may have no choice but to operate in the country, but multinational companies do. Dave Cote, chairperson and CEO of Honeywell, a company with twenty thousand employees in India and an ardent advocate of the country, recently told the *Wall Street Journal*: "Foreign companies are starting to become scared here [in India]. I worry that the Indian bureaucracy is becoming stultifying. I will hire people here, but I will be a lot more reticent about investing in India."[10] Cote's dismay reflects the growing sentiment among global business leaders, who are increasingly disillusioned and pessimistic about India's prospects and rapidly prioritizing investments elsewhere.

It would therefore be logical to conclude that global businesses shouldn't bother with India, at least not in the short run. Or is there something that multinational corporations are missing by jumping to that conclusion?

Win in India to Win Everywhere

The military term *VUCA* means operating in an environment characterized by extreme volatility, uncertainty, complexity, and ambiguity. This term describes well the business environment in India; it should be spelled VUCCA, though, with the addition of another C for corruption.

Interestingly, while India is a VUCCA market, it also represents most other emerging markets. Many countries, especially in Africa, Latin America, and Asia, resemble chaotic India far more than they do centrally directed and efficient China (see figures 1-2, 1-3, and 1-4).

Take corruption; at number 95, India is in the middle of the pack of emerging markets (see figure 1-2). Doing business in these markets means multinational companies have to figure out how to succeed despite rampant corruption. In terms of the ease of doing business, India is a tough place at number 132, but again is highly representative of many other markets, such as Brazil (number 130)

FIGURE 1-2

Global corruption index

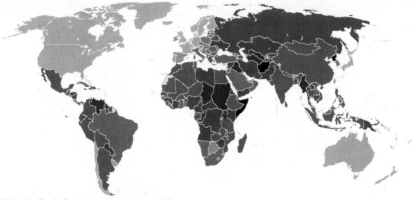

Light shading indicates least corrupt countries
Dark shading indicates most corrupt countries

Source: Reproduced with permission of Transparency International.

FIGURE 1-3

World Bank ranking of countries based on ease of doing business

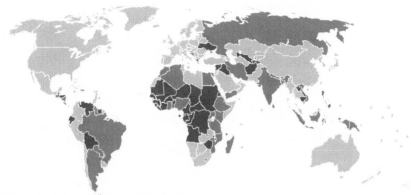

Light shading indicates high ease of doing business
Dark shading indicates low ease of doing business

Source: Wikipedia, see http://en.wikipedia.org/wiki/File:Ease_of_Doing_Business_Index.svg.

FIGURE 1-4

2012 Global Competitiveness Report

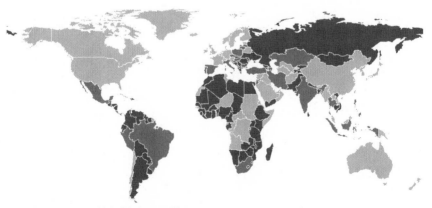

Light shading indicates high global competitiveness
Dark shading indicates low global competitiveness

Source: The Global Competitiveness Network, World Economic Forum, Switzerland, 2012.

and Indonesia (128), according to the World Bank. In the World Economic Forum's *2012 Global Competitiveness Report*, India, at number 59, is just behind Brazil (48) and ahead of Russia (67). Again, most emerging markets, such as Indonesia (50), raise the same issues and challenges as India does.

The inescapable conclusion: doing business in most emerging markets is tough. Frankly, that's why they are called *emerging* markets. Global companies will have to learn how to succeed in those unfamiliar and difficult environments if they want to grow. Both in its potential and in its challenges, therefore, India is an archetype for many emerging markets, especially democratic ones. Moreover, since India offers a market with huge potential, substantial managerial capability, a decent talent pool, and important institutions that many smaller markets lack, it is a good place for multinationals to learn to deal with corruption, volatility, chaos, poor infrastructure, and the problems they will face in other emerging markets.

Succeeding in India will help multinationals build critical capabilities for tomorrow. For example, the structure of demand in India is a flattish pyramid with a fat base. A small affluent segment lies at the top, "the Australia at the top of India," as Steve Ballmer of Microsoft calls it. A quickly growing, middle market segment has the same number of households as Germany and the United Kingdom combined. Tapping that segment represents a big opportunity. Then, there are the 700 million people at the bottom of the pyramid who survive on less than $2 a day (see figure 1-5).

To succeed, a company has to straddle the pyramid. Smart companies start by selling global products at global prices to the top but quickly find a way to crack the middle market. This is not easy, because it requires considerable innovation. Companies have to develop products in India that are disruptive and offer perhaps 70 percent of the value of the global product at 30 percent of the price. Think of $100 smartphones, $2,500 cars, X-ray machines at $400, and

FIGURE 1-5

Indian income pyramid

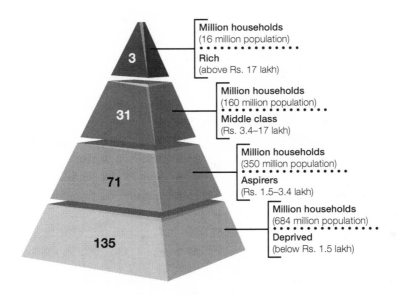

Million households
(16 million population)
Rich
(above Rs. 17 lakh)

Million households
(160 million population)
Middle class
(Rs. 3.4–17 lakh)

Million households
(350 million population)
Aspirers
(Rs. 1.5–3.4 lakh)

Million households
(684 million population)
Deprived
(below Rs. 1.5 lakh)

Entire country stratified by NCAER-CMCR 2010 annual income data

Source: Aresh Shirali, "The Wealth Report," *Open Magazine,* March 12, 2011.

so on. To make money at these price points, companies must localize supply chains and alter business models. They also have to develop deep distribution that reaches into small-town India and build trusted and aspirational brands. Once they succeed, they find that the same offerings and capabilities allow them to win in many other developed and developing countries. Incidentally, the bottom of the pyramid is not about fortunes, but represents an opportunity to earn trust and goodwill through corporate social responsibility and shared value initiatives.

Consider a few examples. Take the case of telecom operator Vodafone, which is India's largest investor. It has had a tough ride into the market with taxation, regulation, and brutal competition, but it has learned to make money in the toughest market in the world, where a phone call costs $0.02 a minute and the average revenue per customer is $3. This has given Vodafone an advantage in many markets in Africa and Europe.[11]

Similarly, for years, tractor manufacturer Deere & Company found it challenging to compete in emerging markets because its giant tractors and harvesters were too large, expensive, and complicated for tiny farms. In 2010, Deere finally developed a compact and affordable thirty-five-horsepower tractor suitable for India. The tractor was developed in India by a team comprising primarily Indian engineers. It's now a big success in India; today Deere exports tractors from its Pune factory to seventy other countries. By taking on rivals in their home markets, companies like Deere and Vodafone have also learned to compete with low-cost, nimble, and entrepreneurial Indian and Chinese challengers.

Hyundai, Suzuki, and Ford have all made India their global hub for small cars. Unilever is repeating its success with low-cost detergents, sachets, and Pureit water purifiers in India in many other developing countries. Both Unilever and Novartis have created new models of distribution to reach less affluent consumers in smaller towns and villages. These channels account for 10 percent of these companies' sales, and they are replicating them in other emerging markets. Unsurprisingly, companies such as Bosch, Dell, Reckitt Benckiser, L'Oréal, Nestlé, Kraft, Schneider Electric, Honeywell, GE, Cummins, and Standard Chartered use India as a proving ground for leaders. They send their stars to India to deliver on tough missions, and Indian stars work overseas, particularly in Southeast Asia and Africa, which are characterized by high growth and volatility.

A number of leaders are beginning to understand that adversity breeds innovation and new capabilities; it's precisely because India is a difficult environment that it is important to learn to succeed here. They see India as a powerful litmus test of their ability to succeed in emerging markets. Shane Tedjarati, president of Honeywell's New Markets, sums it up: "Our success in China and India has created a model that allows us to succeed in Brazil, Africa, and elsewhere." Tim Solso, the former chairman and CEO of Cummins, stated, while announcing a $500 million investment in 2011 that includes three new manufacturing plants and a new R&D center in India: "We are looking at leveraging the capabilities and scale from India to enter Africa."[12] Commenting on the promotion of India President D. Shivakumar as the head of the Middle East, Africa, and India regions, Stephen Elop, Nokia's CEO, said: "India is at the forefront of the company's transition strategy. All our dual SIM launches are doing well, and we are witnessing strong sales. India has shown that brand plus team plus great execution can deliver strong results."[13] Clearly, he expects Shivakumar to replicate Nokia India's success and bring back market share in the ninety countries in those two regions that resemble India.

India's strategic importance is not only because it is a large market; more importantly, it is a laboratory or petri dish for developing products, business models, talent, capabilities, and operating models that will help companies succeed in a host of challenging markets. In the global corporation's architecture, India, along with China, is one of the key hubs for supporting those markets. You have to learn to win in India to be able to win everywhere else.

2

Escaping the
Midway Trap

Obstacles are what you see when you are not focused on the goal.

—OLD INDIAN ADAGE

Many multinational companies are quite pleased with their performance in India. That's because they have set quite a low bar for success. To most, the fact that their business in India is meeting budget or growing at double-digit rates is significant.

But that isn't success. Companies can be growing at double-digit rates and meeting budgets, and still be irrelevant to their parent and in India. McKinsey & Company analysis shows that the twenty-five largest, publicly listed multinational companies in India contributed just 2 percent of their parent's global revenues and profits in 2011.[1] That's telling, especially since many of them have been operating in India for a long time. The Indian operations of companies that have set up shop since 1991 as wholly owned subsidiaries contribute an even more anemic 1 percent of their parent's revenues and profits. If all these operations grow at roughly the same pace as their industry, even after a decade their contribution will still be extremely modest.

Real success in India, I would argue, means meeting three criteria:

1. *The company is a leader in its industry.* That is, it is number one, two, or three in the local market, and gaining market share.

2. *India delivers 10 percent to 20 percent of the company's new growth in revenues and profits on a global basis.* In comparison, China may be delivering 20 percent to −40 percent of global growth.

3. *The company is using India as a hub to win in other markets.* It is taking products developed for India overseas and using the low-cost manufacturing, engineering capabilities, and managerial talent there to support similar markets.

That may seem like a high bar, but some multinational companies have vaulted over it. They span many industries such as banking, engineering, food, packaged consumer goods, trucks, telecom, information technology, and automotive. They are American, South Korean, Japanese, Swedish, French, German, and British. Some are large; others midsize. Yet they are all doing well in India by my parameters. In this book, I will repeatedly refer to this set of winning companies. Despite their diversity, these companies adopt a similar approach:

- The winning companies straddle the pyramid. They don't just stay at the top of the market, but focus on the middle market, developing products tailored for India that span different price points. Volvo, for instance, offers heavy trucks ranging from less than $40,000 to $150,000 under different brands, such as Eicher and Volvo.

- They create a localized business model, including a supply chain that overcomes local challenges and delivers margins even at aggressive price points. A case in point: McDonald's India, which makes money even at the price point of 25 rupees (Rs.) for a burger.

- The winners take a long-term view, trading short-term profits for growth and leadership. They make significant investments in product localization and distribution, and in creating an aspirational brand, ahead of demand and ahead of competitors. For instance, between 1995 and 2005, McDonald's India invested nearly $100 million in setting up a supply chain, creating a brand, and developing a low-cost business model before ramping up its presence across India.

- Smart multinationals run India as a geographic profit center, empowering the local organization to grow the business. They are also quick to localize the top team, reducing their dependence on expatriate managers.

- Finally, they develop the resilience to deal with India's corruption, uncertainty, and volatility, and proactively manage reputations and influence regulations.

Take the case of UK-based construction equipment company JCB. India is the jewel in the JCB crown, contributing over a third of its revenues and perhaps half its global profits. The company has a very substantial share (estimated at 55 percent by industry sources) of the fast-growing Indian construction equipment business, and it is beginning to use its low-cost manufacturing and engineering capabilities to compete in other developing countries. Invigorated by the capabilities it has built in India, JCB has become a global leader in its industry. By contrast, Caterpillar, the world's biggest construction equipment maker, has struggled to get its act together despite being an extremely well-managed company. Caterpillar languishes in fourth position in sales of construction machines in India. In a 2009 interview in the *Financial Times*, then chairman and CEO Jim Owens said he was "disappointed" with Caterpillar's weak showing in India, but was "determined we will do better."[2] Since then, the gap between JCB and Caterpillar in India has only grown bigger. (See "David versus Goliath.")

David versus Goliath: How JCB Created and Dominates the Construction Equipment Industry in India

Anthony Bamford, chairman of UK-based construction equipment manufacturer J C Bamford Excavators Ltd., stood in the sweltering heat of India to watch swarms of workers manually moving tons of earth and stone at a construction site outside Delhi. He was no stranger to the country; this was perhaps his twentieth visit since he first started coming to India as a student in the 1960s and especially after 1979 when JCB established a joint venture (JV) with its Indian partner, Escorts. The JV had done reasonably well, carving out a decent market share in the tiny Indian construction equipment market (approximately the thirtieth largest in the world in 2003). However, Bamford could sense things were changing. The industry was finally beginning to grow at a decent pace, albeit from a tiny base. This had attracted the attention of global leaders, including Caterpillar, Komatsu, Volvo Construction Equipment, and Case New Holland, which had all launched competitive products and were nipping at the heels of the JV. Would JCB be able to ride the construction boom and retain, if not increase, its market leadership?

On the flight back to his home in Gloucestershire, Bamford mulled over what he had seen. Although he had been visiting India for years, he sensed a new dynamism and energy in the air. New construction was beginning everywhere—malls, commercial complexes, homes. The government finally was moving on the big national highway projects. Now a new can-do spirit informed all his meetings, whether with dealers, customers, or even the construction workers he had spoken to. As a result, he sensed that contractors were willing to invest in new machines and new projects.

But was this for real? Over the years, he had seen similar moments of optimism and energy, only to watch India lose steam and disappoint.

Confronted with big opportunities in the United States, China, and Brazil and smaller opportunities in other emerging markets, was it really time to make a big bet on India? He could see that it was not simply a matter of bringing more machines into India. The market in India was fundamentally different. Construction projects were smaller, people had less money to invest, and in most cases, contractors would be buying their first machine ever, having relied for decades on manual labor. The JV would need a simple, inexpensive, and versatile machine instead of sophisticated, costly, and very productive excavators—a Swiss-army knife rather than a more specialized carving knife. Manufacturing would have to be completely localized to keep the pricing competitive. Bamford could see that the dealer network would have to be completely overhauled to provide the kind of customer support and service across India that JCB was famous for globally. He wondered if Escorts, its Indian partner, shared this vision and had the same appetite for investment and growth. The transformation would require strong Indian leadership, a new level of capability on the ground, and much more collaboration between JCB's UK headquarters and India. Most of all, it would require greater engagement and more active sponsorship from him personally. How should he prioritize India over other product and country investment opportunities?

Being a privately held company, JCB was able to move swiftly after Bamford made up his mind to focus on India. The results were impressive. By 2011, revenues had grown nearly fifteen times, and India was now a powerful growth engine for JCB, its largest market worldwide, accounting for about a third of global revenues and perhaps half of its profits. Strategically, JCB had built a dominant market share. The name "JCB" had become synonymous with the industry and virtually the generic term for any construction machine. As the Indian construction equipment market is taking off (it is expected to be one of the top five markets in the world by 2015), JCB is extraordinarily well positioned to ride the wave, while its competitors, including Caterpillar, Komatsu, and Volvo, are scrambling to find a way to participate more effectively. How did JCB do it?

- *Strong and visible leadership commitment to India.* Anthony Bamford, Alan Blake (then head of manufacturing and now the global CEO), and the leadership team at JCB invested time on the ground to understand the market in a nuanced way. They were therefore able to pick up the early signals that drove them to preemptively invest in India and create the market for their machines at a time when India was number 30 in the global construction equipment rankings. JCB competitors under-invested in India. In contrast to JCB, they prioritized India according to the current size of the market rather than the potential size, delegated responsibility for India to midlevel managers in their Asian regional headquarters, and invested in proportion to the size of their existing business rather than the opportunity. More important, leaders at JCB were personally engaged in helping build the business in India; they were deeply involved in developing the dealer network, in product development, in the manufacturing strategy, and in building capability on the ground. Nor did their commitment wax and wane with the ups and downs of the Indian economy; in the middle of the financial crisis of 2008, when most competitors froze their investments in India, not only did JCB carry through with its $100 million manufacturing invest-ment, it also put in a massive equipment-financing program to aid customers and dealers. When demand recovered, JCB was able to dramatically consolidate its leadership.
- *Leveraged global know-how to develop offerings customized for the local market and spanning price points.* Unlike competitors Caterpillar, Volvo, and Komatsu, JCB decided to focus on inexpensive and versatile backhoes, rather than more productive excavators, and in 2005

launched a new model, the 3DX, which went on to become the best-selling construction machine in India. JCB engineers worked hard to adapt the global model for India. While other players optimized their machines for maximum speed and productivity, just as they did in developed markets, JCB optimized machines for fuel efficiency, understanding that this is the biggest driver of operating economics. Over one hundred innovations, small and large, went into making a product that was fully adapted to Indian operation processes and usage conditions. For instance, it brought down the frictional losses in the hydraulic system, modified filtration to handle dusty conditions and the use of diesel adulterated with kerosene, used an aluminum rather than copper radiator to bring down cost, and a heavier bucket. Discovering that many operators are paid by the hour while others are paid by the job, it created two switchable modes of operation, economy and power mode, so that operators could choose when to optimize for fuel efficiency versus productivity. The 3DX was swiftly followed by an explosion of the product range, with a three-ton wheel-loading shovel, a wheel loader, a crane, excavators, and finally a five-ton entry-level backhoe loader—the 2DX—meant for lighter applications in rural India. With twenty-one different machines, JCB offers the broadest product range of any competitor.

- *Localized manufacturing and a robust local supply chain to create a localized business model that delivers good profitability, even at aggressive price points.* JCB was very quick to completely localize its manufacturing in India, including the engine, transmission, and cab. Competitors that hesitated to make this investment ended up with an uncompetitive cost structure and huge exposure to currency fluctuations. Blake and his team made multiple visits to India to get a nuanced understanding of the manufacturing capabilities in the country. Instead of visiting companies with similar low-volume manufacturing processes, they focused on visiting the high-volume plants of Honda, Tata, and LG. They found the capability to be "mindboggling" and well beyond what they had seen, even in the UK. As a result, in 2006, JCB undertook "Project 50" to expand capacity from fifteen backhoes per day to fifty per day, without interrupting production. The success of Project 50 and the market acceptance of the 3DX machine quickly led to Project 100, the creation of the largest backhoe manufacturing facility in the world, with a capacity of a hundred machines a day, with an investment of $100 million. Astonishingly, for a project of this size, it was executed within eight months. The manufacturing innovations were so dramatic that they reduced the assembly time from 105 minutes to 52 minutes. JCB has now replicated these process improvements in the UK and Brazilian factories. As the India team earned its credibility, it attracted further investments. JCB opened a new set of factories outside the city of Pune to focus on heavy machines like excavators and wheel loaders.

- *Invested heavily in building an aspirational brand and a proprietary distribution and service network with deep reach and capability.* Like his father J. C. Bamford, the founder of JCB, Anthony Bamford had a passionate conviction that the right products were merely half the recipe for success. The other part was customer service provided by the dealer network, which by his standards was woeful in both capability and reach in India. JCB India CEO Vipin Sondhi personally drove a focused effort to transform JCB's dealer network, with the support of some of the most experienced service engineers worldwide. JCB established fourteen area offices across India and four training facilities for dealer personnel in each of the four regions. He restructured existing dealerships and added 9 more dealerships and 145 new service points, bringing the total number of dealers to 57 and service centers to 430. (In comparison, Caterpillar has 2 dealers with 112 service points; Komatsu, 25 dealers with 54 service points; and Volvo, 12 dealers with 30 service outlets.) JCB now expected dealers to meet stringent requirements in terms of facilities, equipment, and investment in service engineers to deliver a world-class customer experience anywhere in India. This network runs three hundred customer events and road shows a year versus thirty by the closest competitor. Recognizing that operator training is a huge issue, JCB invested in a residential school for training operators and then showed its dealers how this could be a profitable and loyalty-enhancing new business.

JCB also arranged financing through more than fifty banks and financing companies, enabling thousands of first-time entrepreneurs across the country. Today, over 40 percent of JCB's machines are bought by first-time entrepreneurs. Moreover, unlike most industrial companies, JCB also invested significantly in marketing beyond the usual industry events and road shows. Much like a consumer company, it invested to have a dominant 50 percent share of voice across media channels and signed up Narain Karthikeyan, a young Formula One racing driver, to be its brand ambassador. Across India, buying a "JCB" and becoming an entrepreneur are huge aspirations.

- *Used joint ventures and strategic partnerships to enter the market.* JCB entered India through a joint venture with the Indian company Escorts because regulations required it. The JV was a powerful advantage because it resulted in a completely localized business. The disadvantage was that the JV failed to innovate and improve, and the value of the partnership diminished over time. When strategic objectives began to diverge and regulations allowed, JCB bought out its partner. What JCB did right was not to overly integrate the India business after it became a 100 percent subsidiary; it empowered Escorts to run under a new team.

- *Localized leadership and empowered the local organization to win.* JCB created an entrepreneurial leadership team and empowered it to build the business in a way that made local sense. India is a geographic profit center in JCB, and the India CEO Sondhi reports directly to the global CEO Blake with complete responsibility for the business in India. Accountability for results is ensured through the execution of a rolling three-year plan around which everyone is aligned. Seventy percent of the operating decisions are made locally and the balance, consultatively. Strong local accountability for the business and the traditional JCB value of *jamais contente* (never satisfied)—a sense of urgency about getting things done—has allowed it to be much more agile than competitors that have failed to create local empowerment.

- *Leveraged India for global products, services, and talent.* Having built significant capability on the ground, JCB is now using India to win globally. Exports of components and machines from India are giving it a global cost advantage. JCB is leveraging a large engineering center and success with frugal engineering globally. It is using India to develop global leaders and sending high-potential young Indians to other parts of the world.

The reason some companies are extremely successful in India is simply their extraordinary commitment; this commitment comes from seeing the *potential* of the market rather than its problems. Many years ago, one of my marketing professors told the class the apocryphal story of two shoe salesmen who are sent to Africa. One comes back in despair because he found that Africans don't wear shoes; there simply wasn't a market. The other sent a telegram back, "Natives are friendly STOP No one wears shoes STOP Huge potential STOP Am staying on STOP Send container load of cheap durable sandals END." Companies like Samsung or JCB are winning in India because they are focused on India's potential rather than its many problems. Determined to build a leadership position in what they are convinced will be one of the world's largest markets, they are willing to prioritize India over other markets. They make market-shaping investments and sustain their commitment through the tumultuous cycles of the Indian economy. In the process, they create new markets or categories that they then dominate.

In contrast, their competitors take the same low-risk, low-commitment approach to India as they do to all emerging markets. The strategy in India, as in all markets, is selling to the affluent top of the pyramid, which requires the least adaptation of products, business models, and operating procedures. It is easier to skim the top of the Indian market than to figure out how to crack the challenging middle market. They invest cautiously, in proportion to current revenues rather than the potential. They expect India to operate at the same net profit margin as developed countries, grow profits faster than revenues, and fund most investments out of the annual budget. This, of course, results in systematic underinvestment in anything that has a payback of over a year—building brands or localizing products, for instance. They tightly control employee head count, even if the cost of an employee in India is one-tenth that of an employee in France. The country manager is a midlevel sales executive who reports to the regional sales headquarters, typically Singapore. He or she has to refer most decisions—hiring five people, investing $5,000, offering a 5 percent discount—to someone outside India and spends an enormous amount of time negotiating decisions internally.

For most global small business units (SBUs), India represents about 1 percent of their global revenues, so double-digit growth and the absence of a crisis are celebrated as success. Senior executives, including the CEO, make perfunctory annual visits that are carefully scripted and usually preclude getting a feel for India. According to John Flannery, president of GE India, this approach "has the risk of

FIGURE 2-1

The midway trap

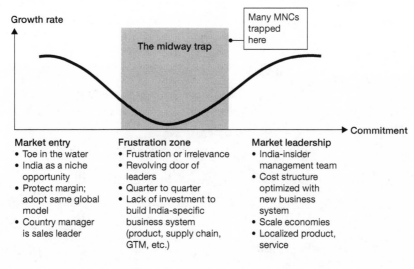

Growth rate

The midway trap

Many MNCs trapped here

Commitment

Market entry
- Toe in the water
- India as a niche opportunity
- Protect margin; adopt same global model
- Country manager is sales leader

Frustration zone
- Frustration or irrelevance
- Revolving door of leaders
- Quarter to quarter
- Lack of investment to build India-specific business system (product, supply chain, GTM, etc.)

Market leadership
- India-insider management team
- Cost structure optimized with new business system
- Scale economies
- Localized product, service

Source: McKinsey & Company Asia Center.

resulting in a low wattage system of low ambition, low commitment, and low energy." As a result, companies end up in the midway trap (see figure 2-1).

Companies find the going good in the first few years after establishing a presence in India. Then they find growth slowing down and face a bigger and bigger challenge to grow faster than the industry average. The small premium segment at the top of the market gets saturated and intensely competitive as every other global company targets the same segment. To continue to grow requires the courage and commitment to move down and compete in the larger middle of the market. However, that requires market-shaping investments in localization and a different operating model. If a company doesn't increase its commitments at this stage, either organically or through acquisitions, it will sink into the midway trap, where growth is determined by the tide of the industry. Even well-managed companies like Caterpillar, Volvo, Microsoft, Procter & Gamble, Nestlé, Dell, and GE have experienced some version of this trap in India.

The Midway Trap at Microsoft India

Microsoft entered India quite early and had built up a reasonable presence by the time I joined the company early in 2004. During his first visit to India on my watch, Steve Ballmer had the insight that there are really three segments in India with an affluent top of the pyramid comprising perhaps 50 million wealthy consumers and 2,500 midsize and large enterprises. This affluent segment is global, using IT devices and software in ways that are similar to customers in developed markets. Microsoft could easily serve this market with the same products, pricing, and go-to-market approach, and the same internal operating model it uses in developed markets. Ballmer felt that Microsoft should first focus on capturing this opportunity, which he called "Australia at the top of the pyramid." Between 2005 and 2009, Microsoft successfully focused on the enterprise segment. As a result, Microsoft India's revenues grew at 30 percent to 50 percent annually and rapidly converged with Microsoft Australia at around US$1 billion. However, once the enterprise segment became saturated, Microsoft found it more challenging to grow much faster than the software industry did.

To sustain leadership, Microsoft India now needs another growth engine. It has to figure out how to tap the middle market, which comprises 8 million small and medium-sized businesses and 50 million middle-class households, which do not use computers. That's a profoundly different market, where the value of using IT is not yet understood. Disposable income is modest, so affordability is a critical issue. The usage of pirated software is over 85 percent. It's a mobile market first, a TV market second, and a PC market third, while Microsoft is still a PC-centric company. In India, customers are spread across three hundred small cities and towns, not conveniently concentrated in the top twenty cities. Broadband connectivity is poor, so penetrating this segment needs a fundamentally different approach—a different value proposition, a different business model that defeats piracy by delivering software as a service through the cloud and offers customers the ability to pay as they go, greater distribution reach, partnerships with telecom operators for connectivity, and so on.

Until Microsoft cracks this proposition, growing much faster than the industry will be a challenge. It could also be vulnerable to a competitor like Google, which might exploit this opportunity faster with little to lose. Conversely, if Microsoft is able to develop a compelling proposition and business model, it could open up large opportunities worldwide. However, figuring out the approach to the mass market requires a very different mind-set and approach and a very different level of commitment to the Indian market. Should Microsoft stay with its standardized model of globalization or double-down on India to extend its early advantage? Making that decision will be part of CEO Ballmer's legacy at Microsoft.

Escaping the Midway Trap

Once a company gets stuck in the midway trap, one of three things usually happens. A few companies like Cummins, GE, P&G, Volvo, and Nestlé dig themselves out of the midway trap and relaunch themselves on a high-growth trajectory. For instance, after a decade of drift, GE India is growing at nearly 50 percent CAGR under India president John Flannery, with the personal commitment of Chairman Jeff Immelt.[3]

Some companies diagnose the slide into the midway trap as a problem with execution or leadership. The solution, they assume, is to change leaders and simply better execute the global play-book. A revolving door of expats ensues, but the results get worse.

Reebok India appears to be in this mode.[4] Others, like pharmaceutical giant AstraZeneca, conclude that the India market is simply too hard or not yet mature, so they invest elsewhere, vowing to be back when the market is more developed, with greater protection for intellectual property (IP), more favorable policies, or better infrastructure. In both cases, the Indian organization is starved of the investments and attention needed to grow faster, and the company will enter a period of drift. Finally, India is consigned to the 1 percent club; the company's market share in India will stay in the low single digits, contributing about 1 percent of global revenues and profits.

These companies are implicitly making a decision to cede India to one or more competitors. Thinking that they will jump back in when the market takes off is an illusion. It's hard to time the market, and in several industries, quite a few companies will already be entrenched. Think how hard it is for Mercedes or Paccar (Kenworth, Peterbilt, and DAF) to catch up in the Indian commercial vehicles sector, where Tata, Leyland, and Volvo have a combined market share of 95 percent, or for Renault to catch up in cars, where Suzuki, Hyundai, Mahindra & Mahindra, and Tata Motors account for 90 percent of sales. It's the same story in many industries, including two-wheelers (motorcycles and scooters), cement, construction equipment, power-generation equipment, and so on. Digging out of the 1 percent club involves fighting a long and costly battle, as Volkswagen and Caterpillar are discovering, or making expensive acquisitions, as pharmaceutical companies have found.[5]

The story of GE's transformation in India shows what it takes to get out of the midway trap. GE has had a presence in India for over seventeen years, but for the most part, GE India is no better than an outpost. Theoretically, GE has virtually everything in its portfolio a growing economy needs, be it consumer appliances, infrastructure, or financial services. Yet GE failed to capitalize on India's economic boom, and its revenues are less than $3 billion; it was therefore a founding member of the 1 percent club. Longtime GE watcher James Schrager, professor of strategic management at University of Chicago's Booth School of Business, remarked: "They have not been successful [in emerging markets], particularly in India which is such a vibrant place. They have been late, flat-footed, and missing what the local market needs."[6]

Several factors contributed to GE's missteps. First, with the exception of its successful JV with Wipro in health care, the other JVs, such as Godrej GE for consumer appliances, HDFC GE for consumer finance, and State Bank of India GE for credit cards, didn't perform well. In the appliance business, for instance, GE lost India to Samsung and LG. Indians didn't want the large refrigerators GE made. In the credit card business, when GE tied up with the State Bank of India (SBI), India didn't have a credit bureau. That meant there was no credit history that companies could rely on to issue cards. SBI suggested GE tap into the thousands of savings accounts SBI managed to vet a customer's track record. "GE just wouldn't accept the idea. They insisted on getting the information from a credit bureau and demanded that SBI stand as guarantor for all the cards issued. You don't ask for such guarantees in the US, why ask for it in India?" recalls a former GE veteran, who steered that business for a while. (Note: The JV with SBI did not perform well historically but with GE's new approach, it has seen a major turnaround in the past two years and is growing rapidly and very profitably.)

Executives at GE India found it exasperating to get headquarters' buy-in for any proposal. "They just couldn't understand that in India, the payback time is longer," says yet another former GE executive who now heads a European company in India. The other mistake, old-timers at GE say, was the company's propensity to send in mid-level executives from other markets to head the India business. India was far more complex than anything those executives had handled, so GE needed more rather than less leadership capability to grow the local market. Schrager points out that the powerful global business units may also have been a challenge:

> Jack Welch made one powerful change in GE, which is to have as small a corporate office as possible. Division presidents run their global business with as little intervention from corporate as possible. The great downside of the vertical system is that the person in charge is very powerful. So if GE, the corporation, wants to go to India, Immelt or whoever is running the place has to go to each president and lobby for that business to go to that place. It's clumsy.

To his credit, CEO Immelt recognized this. In 2009, he drove GE to embrace a radical new organizational model in India. Explaining the changes in an interview with *Forbes India*, he says:

> [Winning in] India is essential. For GE, winning with India requires a new business model, one in which we are "local" in every sense of the word. That means migrating P&L responsibility and major business functions [like R&D, manufacturing and marketing] from a centralized headquarters to an experienced in-country team that is closest to the action and uniquely in touch with local customers and capabilities. Shifting power to where the growth is, putting more resources, more people and more products in the country, and integrating all elements of the GE product and services pipeline makes good business sense. This new One GE in India approach will speed progress. With an integrated team, we can develop products and services designed specifically to meet local needs and, potentially, for export to other markets. Since we've changed the model in India to align with the market more directly, there's great excitement. It gives us entirely new opportunities to develop more products at more price points. This will help open up access to large, underserved markets in India, China, Brazil, and Africa while

also fueling innovation that opens a door into new markets in the more developed regions of the world. The establishment of a new business model in India is an important step and I am eager to see it take off.

The changes in GE's approach to India are profound. For the first time, GE has a senior vice president heading India. Flannery, who was previously the head of GE Capital in Asia, is a trusted veteran with an impressive record. The organization structure has been changed, with all the leaders of businesses and functions reporting to Flannery, who has responsibility for GE India as a profit center and reports to John Rice, a vice chairperson. Flannery and his team have substantial decision rights, including the ability to hire people and invest $250 million over three to five years to build local capabilities.

GE's strategy has shifted to developing more local products for the Indian market and stronger partnerships to gain scale. "We will treat India the same way as we treat any other business in the company," says Guillermo Wille, managing director, John F. Welch Technology Centre (JFWTC), GE's multidisciplinary R&D facility in Bangalore. "This is a big difference for us. Previously, countries were never treated like a business." The idea is that the India team in different businesses will define what products they want and the technology team in Bangalore will develop those products. Adds Flannery:

> One GE is a significant evolution. Our theory is that by concentrating more resources and decision making in India, we will be able to better serve local customer needs and ultimately achieve faster growth. We also hope that by conceiving and developing products for the Indian market, we can in turn use those products to penetrate more mature markets outside of India. We will still have deep connections with our global organization, but the center of gravity will move towards India.

There are significant challenges in implementing the new "One GE" model. Some have to do with building organizational capability in India, like product innovation, supply chain management, and leadership. But the biggest challenges are internal. Says Vijay Govindarajan, a professor at Tuck and an adviser to Immelt: "There are other challenges that will require a mind-set shift. In a HQ-driven company like GE, which is used to working in a certain way, things like reverse innovation and evolving an Indian way to do business will face resistance. It will require decentralization of powers and delegation of authority, which may have some opponents at HQ." The hope is that with Immelt backing the plan, the changes will go through. "There is a realization at the top that people working in emerging markets need to have an explore-and-learn approach. They have to be profitable but not every month. They can spend money, adjust and fine-tune their business model, and then make money," points out Govindrajan. The experiment is in its early stages, but growth is back: GE India is reportedly growing at over 50 percent annually.

Why Is It So Hard to Change?

Why is it so hard to avoid the midway trap? Why is it even harder to escape it, once trapped? The prescriptions for success in India are hardly rocket science, and companies are filled with extremely bright people. These questions were the most difficult to answer. As it turns out, they're fundamentally about corporate mind-sets.

The world is quietly entering a new era or phase of globalization, which is happening in an unheralded and therefore more dangerous way (I describe the new era in chapter 9). With the economies of the developed world in trouble, multinational companies increasingly have to look for growth in developing markets. So far, what has passed for globalization is international expansion of companies from the affluent world, growing their presence across developed countries and then across the developing world. Their success has come largely from an export-driven approach in which they targeted the affluent in every country and replicated their products, business models, and management systems and practices across countries. However, this model of skimming the top has limits. It is less successful in reaching the next billion emerging middle-class customers who are far less affluent and who live in countries that, like India, have poor infrastructure, skill shortages, rampant corruption, and very high volatility and uncertainty.

Cracking this segment requires a new model of globalization that is radically, not incrementally, different. In a prescient article in *Harvard Business Review*, the late C. K. Prahalad wrote:

When large Western companies rushed to enter emerging markets 20 years ago, they were guided by a narrow and often arrogant perspective. They tended to see countries like China and India simply as targets—vast agglomerations of would-be consumers hungry for modern goods and services. This "corporate imperialism" has distorted the operating, marketing, and distribution decisions multinationals have made in serving developing countries. In particular, these companies have tended to gear their products and pitches to small segments of relatively affluent buyers—those who, not surprisingly, most resemble the prototypical Western consumer. They have missed, as a result, the very real opportunity to reach much larger markets further down the socioeconomic pyramid. Succeeding in these broader markets requires companies to spend time building a deep and unbiased understanding of the unique characteristics and needs of developing countries and their peoples. But such time is well spent. Not only will it unlock new sources of revenue, it will also force big companies to innovate in ways that will benefit their operations throughout the world.[7]

However, the mind-set and behavior change that Prahalad refers to is a paradigm shift, which is, by definition, destabilizing and threatening. Think about the implications of the new model. The dominant hub-and-spoke architecture of a company with an all-knowing, all-powerful headquarters instructing and supervising the geographical subsidiaries gives way to a new architecture of multiple hubs, including China and India, that is run as real profit-and-loss businesses with significant operating freedom. Innovation happens not just in product divisions and at headquarters but in geographic areas, too. Executive leaders don't just live at headquarters; many operate out of hubs. The company has to cut investments in the rich, slowing markets of Europe and in product divisions or strategic business units in order to fund investments in key emerging markets. It also has to have the patience and tenacity to wait for these investments to pay back. It has to prioritize markets, not on the basis of revenues but on opportunity. This requires new capabilities, such as the ability to operate in places that are corrupt, volatile, and uncertain. The company has to behave with humility, responsibility, and open-mindedness in all countries. Poor safety and environmental practices, monopolistic pricing, and the dumping of obsolete or banned products in emerging markets won't go unchallenged.

No wonder it's easier to be an ostrich and simply execute the old model better.

Companies often tread cautiously and reluctantly in markets like India. The reluctance could prove costly. Many industry leaders could be replaced by smaller competitors or newer players from emerging markets that embrace the next wave of globalization faster. Paradigm shifts invariably reorder leadership; incumbent leaders are slower to adapt than hungry underdogs or new players. Just think of how Apple, Google, and Samsung have devastated Nokia and Research In Motion and put Microsoft on the defense. Or going back in time, how Japanese firms challenged Detroit and consumer electronics giants like GE, Phillips, and Thompson. In a similar way, companies like Samsung, Hyundai, Cummins, JCB, Nestlé, Schneider Electric, Unilever, and Standard Chartered Bank are quietly creating new growth engines and unassailable leadership positions in places like India and paving the way for industry leadership.[8]

Because the changes we are talking about are deep and affect the DNA and operating system of companies, to have any chance of success at all, they cannot be delegated to leaders who operate within rigid frameworks. In most companies, globalization is the responsibility of a president of sales or a senior vice president for international business. The mandate of these leaders is simply to grow the business by selling more stuff around the world. It is not within their remit to challenge the investment process or the innovation process. The only place where it all comes together is the corner office, which is why the CEO has to champion the strategy to win in India and other emerging markets and the board has to explicitly support it. Leadership in emerging markets becomes a defining choice for today's CEOs.

The prognosis is not good. Most senior leaders in multinational companies have their experience base in the developed world; they lack a feel for and understanding of emerging markets. Many don't even like emerging markets—noisy, chaotic, corrupt places that don't play by Western rules. It's a tall order to expect a CEO who brings his or her familiar food on the corporate jet to see the potential of these markets.

CEO tenures are also declining. According to a recent Conference Board survey, tenures are now shorter than seven years. Very often, building leadership in India can take a decade. It's a rare CEO who is willing to pay the price by investing on his or her watch, knowing that the credit might well go to a successor.

Obsession with China at the expense of India is another major issue. While every CEO acknowledges that it's all about China and India, the reality is that the rise of China has caused many CEOs to overlook India. In the short term, China looks like a much greater opportunity.

However, a comparison of the profitability of foreign companies in China and India suggests that on a risk-adjusted basis, the differences may not be quite as large.

To be fair to today's CEOs, they have an incredibly tough job, with the world's major economies in trouble, more regulatory challenges, more competition, more pressure from Wall Street, and so on. In the middle of all that, we are asking them to prioritize winning in emerging markets, with India as a lead market, at a time when India is presenting itself in a spectacularly poor light.

The Levers of Success

CEO commitment is the starting point. In India, winning requires a very different business leader—an entrepreneurial general manager rather than a salesperson and, ideally, a senior and trusted insider with credibility and influence. It requires a different organizational structure or model, where India is managed like a geographic profit center, with the ability to make important operating decisions without enormous negotiations and persuasion. It needs a willingness to make long-term investments in developing capabilities on the ground and the willingness to sustain these through the inevitable vicissitudes. Therefore, escaping the midway trap requires the commitment of the entire leadership of the company to pull multiple levers before the whole organization flips to a new high-growth trajectory.

In the rest of the book, I will delve into issues that determine a company's success in India. The single most important determinant of success over time is the choice of the country manager. What is the role of the country manager in India? Why is it different from that of the country manager of, say, Germany? What kind of person should be in the role? I discuss these issues in chapter 3.

What kind of an operating model do you need to be successful in India? How do you achieve speed without taking undue risks? What is the new role of headquarters? Are there any principles for strategy that are common across industries and companies? How do you get the whole organization aligned behind a strategy for India? These are the topics in chapter 4.

In chapter 5, I discuss how to build the leadership and organizational capabilities to succeed, and why that is so hard for most companies. I will also describe some best practices.

Chapter 6 is devoted to India as a lab for innovation. Why is that critical? How hard is it? Who is doing it well? What can we learn from these companies?

In chapter 7, I cover questions about joint ventures and acquisitions. After analyzing why they have a bad reputation, we will find out what we can learn from companies that are good at JVs and acquisitions.

Chapter 8 is all about developing the resilience to deal with corruption and cope with chaos.

In chapter 9, the focus is on the role of the global CEO. Why do you need a globalizer and how do you identify this archetype? What do the most successful globalizers do to ensure leadership in India and China?

And, finally, in chapter 10, I will show how companies that are winning in India are learning to use the capabilities they have developed there to break into several emerging markets.

THE TAKEAWAYS

- With the exception of a few industries, India is strategically vital for most MNCs. Despite many challenges, India's fundamentals will likely make India one of the largest markets worldwide in the next two decades. With China and Brazil already emerging, India may be the last giant market where an MNC can still aspire to build a dominant position. Even more important, India represents many emerging markets, both in consumer behaviors and market structure and in challenges such as corruption, uncertainty, and poor infrastructure. Winning in India becomes a test of a company's ability to succeed in emerging markets. India, with China, should be a hub or platform of products, talent, and capabilities for serving other emerging markets that lack the scale and capability.

- The biggest determinant of a company's success in India is CEO commitment and engagement. Succeeding in India requires that companies think, organize, and operate very differently than they currently do. This is not an incremental shift. It represents a paradigm shift that requires a fundamental reprogramming of mind-sets, operating routines and the governance model, new capabilities, and different leadership. It therefore needs the CEO's hands-on leadership; change management cannot be delegated to roles such as the head of sales or the president of international business.

- Deciding to look past the chaos and challenges of India and build a leadership position in what is or will be one of the world's largest markets is a defining choice for boards and CEOs.

- In the absence of commitment, companies frequently fall into the midway trap, where they can grow no faster than the industry average and are restricted to the tiny premium segment at the top of the market. They end up in the 1 percent heap, where India continues to contribute just 1 percent of global revenues and the company has an irrelevant 1 percent (or low single-digit) share of one of the largest markets in the world. Catching up once the market takes off will be expensive, since both foreign and Indian competitors will likely have built up entrenched leadership positions.

3

The Country Manager in India

I cannot emphasize enough getting the right leadership in India. The only time we have made progress is when we had the right set of Indian leaders in the top jobs, fully aligned with our strategy. Anything less resulted in chaos or drift.

—TIM SOLSO, FORMER CHAIRMAN AND CEO, CUMMINS INC.

Getting the right leader on the ground is unquestionably the single most important determinant of a company's success in India. Although many executives don't explicitly realize it, global leaders' commitment to India is inextricably linked to the level of their trust and confidence in the country head, with the right leader triggering a spiral of good performance and commitment. However, choosing a country manager is a complicated decision that most companies struggle to get right.

The choices are many and confusing. What do you look for? An Indian or an expat? What's more important, an understanding of India and the local market or of the company? Do you look for an execution genius, an entrepreneurial builder, or an ambassador? What matters more: industry knowledge or leadership ability? Do you put in a high-potential young Turk or a seasoned, senior leader? Consequently, the choice of country manager is frequently a process of trial and error, and success is often driven more by chance than understanding. Many companies drift through a revolving door of leaders or an overdependence on expats. The consequences are costly.

As a country manager, as well as a leader of country managers, I have witnessed many successes and failures. In this chapter, I will draw on my personal experiences as well as those of several other country managers to demystify the job.

Choosing the Country Manager

Match the profile to the job. This sounds obvious, but it isn't. A company's journey in India usually proceeds through several distinct phases. The first is when the company enters the market. The mission is incubation. The priorities are to establish a sales and marketing organization, distribution channels, and channel partners; achieve a basic level of localization of the product; and put in the basic infrastructure and functional processes and controls. The strategy at this phase is often simple: sell global products at global prices to the affluent global segment. Since the capabilities on the ground are limited, the support and oversight of a mature regional organization, typically in Singapore or Hong Kong, are vital.

The likely profile of the country leader for this mission is a young, driven, high-potential, sales-oriented leader of high integrity, unfazed by ambiguity and strong in execution, who can be developed over time into a competent general manager. A country head who is Indian, with knowledge of the market and Indian business practices, is a big advantage at this stage.

The leadership challenge emerges when the company has drifted into the midway trap that I described in the previous chapter and has to play catch-up or when it senses a bigger opportunity. Many companies currently confront this dilemma. To identify the right leaders, they need to learn from companies in India that have successfully made the transition to the second phase, such as Samsung, Pepsi, JCB, Nokia, Cummins, GE, Nestlé, and Schneider Electric.

The mission at this phase, to build leadership in the large but challenging middle market, is not easy. It is a very different game. Companies have to become local in their operations and act much more like an Indian company, but still leverage global brands, platforms, capabilities, and resources. The country leader's challenge is to be ambidextrous: execute the top of the pyramid model and entrepreneurially grow in the middle market at the same time.

Over the past two years, I have studied several country managers who have led the charge. For instance, Vipin Sondhi has led a transformation at JCB, the dominant player in the Indian construction equipment industry, since 2005. GE India's John Flannery is leading the company out of the midway trap. Schneider Electric's Olivier Blum has overseen growth catalyzed by five acquisitions and a joint venture that have created multiple brands, thirty-one factories, one thousand engineers, and seventeen thousand employees in five short years. And Nokia's D. Shivakumar was instrumental in the company's gain of a dominant 60 percent share of the Indian mobile handset market between 2004 and 2008 (although Nokia has subsequently lost share due to a combination of global factors).

The distinguishing characteristic of all such leaders is that they are trusted, senior, entrepreneurial, and general managers, not midlevel sales managers or functional leaders. They are, of course, good at execution; you have to be good at execution to deliver budgets and results predictably, despite the volatility of India. Therefore, they lead from the front and drive their teams hard. Through personal example and emotional connection, they inspire people to stretch, strive, and excel. They have a sense of urgency, drive accountability, and make decisions quickly. They have a low tolerance for bureaucracy and keep things simple. They have a strong sense about what things really matter and stay ruthlessly focused on them despite the many distractions.

However, good country managers are more than execution geniuses. They operate like general managers, not functional leaders. They have an end-to-end view of the business and think not just about sales, but also the balance sheet and the bottom line, about investments, revenues, expenses, margins, cash flow, and returns. They balance short-run priorities with medium- and long-term ones rather than worrying only about the quarter. They are acutely aware that short-term results are vital to bootstrap commitment and investments, but pay attention to longer-term priorities such as growing talent and organizational capabilities as well.

These leaders have the ability to sense and paint a picture of the massive opportunity in India. This is not the usual macroeconomic description of India with hackneyed phrases, like the "demographic dividend," but a granular view of where the growth lies: which segments, which accounts, what channels, what partnerships, and what changes are needed in the global operating and business models to succeed in this market. These CEOs are effective in persuading corporate stakeholders to allow experimentation that demonstrates proof of concept: a small acquisition, a new product, a regional success. They use these first wins to earn confidence and set off a spiral of investment, empowerment, and growth. In that sense, they operate not unlike a venture-backed start-up in the context of a large company.

A transformational deal or opportunity is sometimes more effective than a strategic plan in getting headquarters' attention. "Bring me a deal I can get excited about rather than a strategy," Kevin Johnson, my boss at Microsoft and now CEO of Juniper Networks, once advised me. His advice was sound; entrepreneurial country managers should be able to bring such a game-changing deal to the table. To do this, they have to understand the market from a customer's perspective, have an end-to-end understanding of the company's offerings, possess entrepreneurial flair and the ability to sell ideas internally as well as externally, and lead global teams by influence rather than authority. Shane Tedjarati, Honeywell's president for all high-growth markets, explains that in China and India, game-changing opportunities often present themselves in unique ways: they are without precedent and cut across a company's offerings. The country manager has to be creative in packaging the company's offerings and capabilities into a winning proposal. Imagine the opportunity for the IBM India head in 2003 when one of the world's largest mobile cellular network operators, Bharti Airtel, told him that it wanted to outsource its entire IT infrastructure, but expected the winning vendor to enter into a long-term partnership, invest hundreds of millions of dollars, share risks, and be prepared to earn a fraction of a cent for a minute of talk time!

In those situations, a country manager has to assemble a cross-functional, cross-business unit team, imaginatively structure a proposal, identify risks, and sell the idea to diverse stakeholders in the company, while racing against aggressive rivals. The stakes are high; such a deal sets a precedent, and the winner takes many of the subsequent contracts by leveraging its experience. IBM India, for instance, has won eight out of ten outsourcing contracts in India on the back of its Airtel deal.

Meanwhile, the country manager in India has to deal with large gaps in people's capabilities. His or her counterpart in the United Kingdom would likely have a seasoned team, with depth in marketing and supply chain management as well as leaders who can manage a $100 million business without too much hand-holding. This is not be the case in India, where, because of the lack of seasoned talent, the country manager has to be much more versatile and hands-on, and understand nearly every function. He or she also has to spend a disproportionate amount of time and effort on building a strong leadership team and a capable organization. Successful country managers prioritize this above all else, especially in the first three years of their tenure. As Tedjarati puts it, "I pulled one lever more than anything else, and that was the people lever. Above all, I was the company's Chief People Officer."

The final element in the profile of a country manager is trust. The physical and cultural distance of the headquarters from India and the high levels of corruption in the country, coupled with the need to operate differently in India, put a premium on trust. Trust has several dimensions. At the most basic, given the risk of corruption and fraud in India, the country manager must be a person of impeccable honesty and integrity. A second aspect is good judgment; many situations that arise require an immediate response based on sound common sense. These decisions can't be made in Singapore or Paris. The company has to be able to count on the country head to do the right thing in every circumstance. Third, as Tim Solso of Cummins says, trust means knowing that the country manager is implementing the global strategy and isn't pursuing a different agenda. Finally, there must be confidence in the country manager's ability to execute well. There are many advantages to having a senior leader with a track record in the company and a network, who wields respect, influence, and authority at headquarters. For instance, Nestlé's Helio Waszyk ran an R&D center in Vevey before moving to India. His ability to walk into the CEO's office and argue the need to set up an R&D center in India gives him an edge over even exceptional outsiders. Similarly, in selecting senior GE veteran John Flannery to head the business in India, Jeff Immelt explained that "it is absolutely necessary that the leader of our new organization [in India] has an outstanding track record in the company."

At the same time, a perpetual dependence on expats at the top isn't healthy. French, South Korean, and Japanese companies in particular seem reluctant to trust Indians for the top job. That could become problematic; LG and Samsung have found it hard to attract Indian talent, and Suzuki doesn't have a single Indian on its executive board, leading to speculation that some of its recent labor problems may have cultural roots. Solso agrees: "One mistake was too many expats at certain times in our history. They did serious damage because they did not have a clue as to what was going on from both a business perspective as well as culturally. I would emphasize a limited number of expats and not in the top job; everyone knows they will go back to their country of origin and will wait them out." Thus, the top priority, as the success of companies like Cummins, Unilever, Bosch, and Standard Chartered in India suggests, must be to grow a no-compromise leader who both is a trusted insider and understands India.

The Country Ambassador versus the Country Manager

Some companies experiment with an interesting profile: a country chairperson who is a weak overlay over the business and largely plays an ambassadorial role. However, statesmanship and ambassadors are best left to the realm of diplomacy. These roles are a legacy of an era that no longer exists. GE tried the model over the past decade with limited success and finally abandoned it. A ceremonial role, with no accountability for the business and the responsibility only for engaging government, industry associations, and other CEOs, is usually not effective. Everyone—employees, customers, business partners, government officials—will quickly see this role for what it is and dismiss the person as lightweight. This does disservice to the incumbent and the role.

The ambassadorial country manager who smells opportunity, but is powerless to act, can become intensely frustrated. Increasingly, the connections among strategy and execution, business, reputation, and regulation are tightening, so an artificial separation of these functions is suboptimal. Bringing accountability for these together in a single leader is vital for growing competent and well-rounded business leaders, who are capable of even being the CEO someday.

If the business does require wise counsel, access, and influence and a senior public face, a strong advisory board headed by an iconic leader who serves as a nonexecutive chairperson may be a more prudent approach. We followed this model at Microsoft India with considerable success; the approach is gaining popularity at companies like Coca-Cola, Schneider Electric, and JCB.

The Country Manager's Traits and Competencies

In 2010, I had to accept the fact that I had made a major hiring mistake. I was disappointed because everyone had had huge hopes for this high-profile hire, an incredibly accomplished and successful person. I was personally responsible for hiring this leader and had followed a textbook process, yet the outcome had turned out to be poor. It forced me to look back at my record of promoting and hiring senior leaders, including several country heads.

On one hand, I had helped develop at least twenty-five leaders who were either CEOs or running major divisions of companies in India by then. However, my batting average with senior hires was only 50 percent. I was clearly better at growing than hiring top executives, so I decided to work on my hiring ability by reflecting on my own decisions, by talking to the best executive recruiters in the world, and by interviewing a few leaders and leadership gurus. My aim was not to develop a robust new leadership model; plenty exist.[1] Nor was it to propose a comprehensive new approach to executive recruitment.

My objective was to see if some attributes correlated highly with the success of senior leaders in India. I eventually identified five attributes that make a difference. Being rigorous about these when hiring has made an enormous difference to my success in recruiting senior leaders.

When hiring senior business leaders such as country managers, it is common practice to use a standard set of competencies. The list is usually long and includes familiar attributes such as drive for results, execution ability, strategic thinking, customer centricity, business acumen, and people and team leadership. These may all good things to look for, but I have found that paying attention to three traits (courage, higher ambition, and entrepreneurship) and two competencies (learning agility and people skills) greatly improved my own record. Let me explain.

The Key Traits of Country Managers

Courage may be the most important, scarce, and overlooked leadership characteristic. People often emphasize authenticity and integrity, but courage seems more fundamental. By courage, I mean the ability to think through complex situations and do what is right rather than what is convenient or expedient. It is the ability to take calculated risks and ask for forgiveness rather than permission. It is taking personal responsibility for decisions and results, rather than blaming circumstances or others.

Such courage is a central characteristic of outstanding country managers and, indeed, all leaders. That's particularly important in India, because situations will arise almost every week to test a country head. I recall several occasions when, in retrospect, I wish I had shown greater courage. For instance, early in my career, I was the head of a joint venture in which the agreement was one-sided; all start-up losses were the responsibility of one partner, while profits were equally shared. The agreement was wrong, it rankled our Indian partner, and it was therefore untenable in the long run. Had I shown more leadership in calling this a bad agreement and renegotiating it, I would have won more trust and respect from our partner. Instead, I took no responsibility for it and allowed matters to come to a head. We recovered from that, rebuilt trust, and the joint venture has been successful ever since. But my own behavior bothered me. Why did I hesitate? Because it would have been extremely unpopular in the organization I worked for; my managers might have concluded that I had gone native and trusted me less, which might have affected my career. These worldly considerations took precedence over doing what in my heart I knew to be right.

That taught me a powerful lesson, which I tried to absorb. Many years later, another situation arose when one of our senior leaders concluded a deal with a major Indian customer. The global business refused to honor the deal because the Indian executive had exceeded her empowerment. This quickly became an issue of trust; how could the customer trust a company that wouldn't stand behind a commitment from a senior manager? It would have been easy to hide behind the usual smokescreen of policies, empowerment limits, and so on. However, the old lesson was fresh in my mind and I summoned the courage to cut through the bureaucracy and appeal to the global CEO. Thanks to his intervention, the company eventually stood by the agreement, which laid the foundation of a major partnership in India.

There are many instances like this when country managers have to put their careers on the line and do what is right. For instance, they may have to stand up to headquarters and resist global edicts that make no sense in India, such as cutting 10 percent of the workforce when the local market is growing at double-digit rates or refusing to hire a candidate recommended by a senior politician. They may also have to stand up for employees who may have angered visiting executives or terminated competent leaders whose values didn't fit those of the organization.

How do you look for evidence of courage? It's a huge advantage if the person is already an employee; you can observe behavior and know what his or her peers and subordinates think. In external hiring, the interview and reference checks must zero in on the issue with questions such as: Can you tell me about a situation where you showed uncommon courage? What choices did you face? What was your dilemma? How did you act? Why did that require courage? What were the consequences? What did you learn? The depth and realism of the answers will be revealing.

Higher ambition is the second key trait of a country manager—the extraordinary inner drive to create something larger than oneself. In hiring leaders, we invariably look for traits like passion, hunger, and drive for results. The absence of passion and drive is a dampener, but the drive for results by itself is not enough. It often turns out to be little more than a vehicle for personal ambition, which can have disastrous impacts on people and the culture and, in extreme cases, may result in fraud and wrongdoing.

Passion must emanate from a desire to create something bigger than oneself, one's career, and short-term business results—what academics call higher ambition.[2] The ambition can simply be to create a wonderful workplace that unleashes human spirit and the potential of employees, to become the best factory in India, or to solve tough societal problems through innovation. Such ambition connects the day-to-day activities of employees with a higher purpose that inspires people, especially the younger generation.

The millennials (those born between 1980 and 2000) supposedly lack loyalty, focusing on entitlements and rewards, but I find many young Indians hungry for meaning and purpose. For instance, Microsoft India's computer literacy program, one of the initiatives constructed as part of the company's mission to transform society through computers, was a source of inspiration to most employees. Higher ambition therefore matters when it comes to hiring talent and unleashing commitment. It is also critical for building trust with government, nongovernmental organizations, media, and other stakeholders that are suspicious of business in general and the motivations of multinational companies in particular. A country leader who sees business as a vehicle for changing people and transforming society will be able to establish trust more quickly.

Finally, higher ambition is a vital source of energy and affirmation for the leader. Building an important presence in India is a mission that can take a country manager five to ten years to accomplish. Longevity and tenure are therefore critical. Tedjarati of Honeywell says, "You want executives who are thrilled to have this job and see the job in India as the endgame. You want a leader who sees this as the Big Job, not someone who is impatient to tick the box and sees India merely as a ticket to the Big Job."

However, being a country manager in India isn't easy. It is enormously draining to be sandwiched between the bureaucracy of the country and the company. Many country managers therefore see the role as a three-year assignment: In year one, goes the joke, they unpack. In year two, they deliver an unsustainable spike in performance. In year three, they pack and head off to their next job, leaving a mess that their successor has to clean up. Spending five or ten years in the same role involves short-term career sacrifices, as peers, who stay close to headquarters or change roles frequently, will move faster up the ladder. The motivation that comes from serving a higher purpose then becomes important and enables country managers to stay and build institutions and leave a legacy.

The final trait that is important in a successful country head is *entrepreneurship*. Having discussed that earlier in this chapter, I won't repeat myself. Suffice it to say that multinational companies must appoint leaders who have a keen sense for market opportunities and entrepreneurially build profitable businesses by leveraging the company's global assets.

The Core Competencies

Consider the situations that a country leader in India routinely has to deal with:

- A Maoist insurgency in central India has delayed road transport. It will take weeks, instead of days, for deliveries of components and finished products.

- An abrupt change in the government's policy on taxes causes confusion. No transactions can take place for weeks until the policy is clarified.

- An assessing officer changes the interpretation of the tax code retroactively, so the company is technically now a tax evader. That's a criminal offense, and the legal notice holds you personally accountable as CEO.

- A state government takes nine months to refund local taxes and headquarters wants to write it off as a bad receivable. Unfortunately, the sum represents 4 percent of annual revenues.

- Your public-sector business has come to a standstill, with fear of corruption scandals and investigations paralyzing officials.

- A builder who is also a prominent politician refuses to refund the deposit on an office the company had leased.

- Massive power cuts follow a weak monsoon, and captive generation capacity is inadequate. The wait time for new generators is six months.

- Politicians call for a *bandh* or twenty-four-hour shutdown. The employees in the 24/7 support center can't get to work, so customers in the United States won't be happy.

- When a popular movie star dies of old age, people go berserk with grief. A city of 7 million grinds to a halt, and the windows of your corner office are smashed.

Given such extraordinary uncertainty and volatility, *learning agility* is an essential leadership competency in India. Organizations such as the Center for Creative Leadership and Korn/Ferry describe learning agility as the ability, when thrown into a situation unlike any a person has ever encountered, to learn quickly from experience, succeed, and then apply the learning to perform successfully in other radically new situations. It is the ability to learn quickly in real time, combined with resilience and tenacity to work through big challenges.

Instead of becoming intimidated, agile learners thrive in difficult situations. They are critical thinkers who examine problems carefully and make fresh connections between causes. They are reflective, self-aware, and curious. They like to experiment with change, can deal with the resulting discomfort, and deliver results through team building and personal drive. Humility in success, courage in the face of failure, and willingness to learn from failure are hallmarks of such leaders. There is compelling evidence to show that learning agility, rather than past performance, is the best indicator of leadership potential. Warren Bennis says: "The signature skill of great leaders is the ability to process new experiences ... and to integrate them into their lives. They look at the same events that unstring those less capable ... and see something useful."[3]

In dynamic environments like India's, it becomes critical to assess leaders' learning agility. Firms like Korn/Ferry have developed assessment tools to measure this ability on subdimensions, such as mental, people-related, change, and results agility. These assessments are quite accurate in their diagnostic and predictive powers. I recommend their use both during hiring and for leadership development. Learning agility is a capability that can be strengthened by experience, by repeatedly throwing young leaders into ever more complex and difficult challenges, a point I will pick up in a later chapter.

People skills are the second competency country managers must have. Academics like Daniel Goleman define it more precisely as *emotional intelligence*. People skills are important for every manager, but the country manager in India has to be, frankly, pretty amazing at handling people. Focusing just on business is unlikely to produce great results; taking the time to get to know people well matters for success.

India is a country where an enormous amount is done on the strength of relationships with customers, with government, and with suppliers and dealers. If there is a personal relationship, miracles happen. Customers will place an order to help you meet your budget or release a payment despite a cash crunch. A supplier will prioritize capacity in a time of shortage. Government officials might go out of their way to help resolve a problem because of a relationship. A politician might help during a labor dispute. An industry association might take up your policy issue with the government. And so on. Without relationships, every one of these can become a problem, so the country manager's responsibility is to build a network of important relationships.

It's also necessary to manage people at headquarters. Despite the professionalism of multinationals and their organization charts, job descriptions, and processes, ultimately things are done because of relationships, trust, and goodwill. Many country managers view managing the global matrix as a frustrating part of the job and quickly tire of it. Successful country managers understand the importance of having a strong internal network, so they invest a fair amount of time building personal relationships with the CEO and senior leaders as well as middle managers, who have the power to thwart or enable decisions. They build relationships across functions, especially risk management functions that have a lot of veto power, such as finance, legal, taxation, and real estate. They share many meals, they educate, they invite people to visit India, and they are sure to thank, praise, and recognize good work and help. That's not an act; it is simply part of their nature.

Finally, managing an organization within India itself also requires terrific people skills. Employees in India have a high need to feel an emotional connection with their leaders. Leaders of Indian family businesses understand this all too well, but professionally run companies turn out to be impersonal places, leaving employees hungry for connection. Effective country managers find many ways, spontaneous and planned, to connect with their people. They are also good teachers. In an emerging market like India, capabilities and maturity are often modest; a good leader has to use every interaction as a teaching moment to build the culture.

Successful country managers build great teams around themselves. They expend extraordinary effort in creating a passionate and cohesive leadership team. They hold the bar high on performance and even higher on values and make difficult decisions about who should stay or go. They show no reluctance in hiring people smarter than they are, give them big jobs, and offer them huge challenges. They invest heavily in building trust, creating cohesion, and instilling a sense of mission.

Claudio Fernández-Aráoz, a senior leader in search firm Egon Zehnder's Buenos Aires office, has compared 227 highly successful executives with 23 who failed in their jobs. He found that the managers who failed usually had high expertise and IQs, but in every case, their fatal weakness was in emotional intelligence—arrogance, overreliance on IQ, inability to adapt, and disdain for collaboration or teamwork, and a very cold transactional approach with people.[4]

Many leaders in India, rising through a quasi-Darwinian intellectual culling of the weak, can be high in IQ and drive but have limited emotional intelligence. It is easy for them to fall into these traps.

There is also another risk. In a hierarchical and sycophantic society like India, it's easy for such a leader to start feeling like a god and see leadership as a set of entitlements, rather than responsibilities. Over fifteen years, I have seen many talented leaders crash and burn because things went to their heads, impairing judgment, making them arrogant and out of touch, and costing them trust, followership, and, eventually, their careers.

Growing Global Leaders in India

People often ask me why these qualities—courage, high ambition, entrepreneurship, learning agility, and good people skills—are unique to country managers in India. They are not; these are essential ingredients of leadership everywhere. It's just that India is such a demanding place that the leadership challenge is much greater than most other roles. In addition, along with China, India is often a microcosm of the entire company. All the divisions, products, and solutions of the company and all the functions, ranging from R&D to IT, are likely to be present. The India manager's role is therefore a good test and an incubator of leadership, entrepreneurship, and general management ability.

Recognizing this, several global CEOs see India as an incubator for the next generation of senior leaders, perhaps even the next CEO. Many companies, like Unilever, Ericsson, Schneider Electric, and Reckitt Benckiser, use India to accelerate the development of talented executives in their late thirties or early forties, who have the potential to be on the company's leadership team. Jean-Pascal Tricoire, CEO of Schneider Electric, unequivocally says it is highly unlikely that his successor would not have cut his or her teeth in China or India.

HOW HEADQUARTERS CAN HELP COUNTRY MANAGERS SUCCEED. It is not enough to hire a great country leader with the right stuff; multinational companies need to do all they can to help local leaders thrive. First, they must make the job attractive to the best and brightest. For instance, the Indian subsidiary should be a geographic profit center, with significant decision rights. The job level should be a function of the size of the opportunity, not the size of the business. The incumbent should be able to grow with the business for between five and ten years without having to leave India to boost his or her career.

Second, the India and China country managers should report to a member of the top management team who has lived in and built a business in an emerging market, like Walmart's Scott Price, Honeywell's Shane Tedjarati, or Standard Chartered's Jaspal Bindra. Leaders who have worked only in developed markets and have little empathy for emerging markets can be unintentionally dysfunctional. He or she should not be simply a hard-driving salesperson, but a strategic manager who is capable of reframing the company's aspirations for India and aligning the global system behind them. He or she should also be capable of creating an environment in which leaders can flourish.

Third, multinational companies must assign mentors to country managers. The counsel of a leader who has the full strategic picture and the ear of the CEO and other senior leaders is extraordinarily helpful. I was fortunate to have people like Joe Loughrey, Cummins's chief operating officer, and Craig Mundie, Microsoft's chief technology officer, as mentors. In companies like Nokia, Renault, and Ericsson, the global CEO makes it a point to engage regularly with the country heads of important countries like India. These connections are vital for getting a sense of market opportunities and spotting stresses in the system. They also boost the self-confidence and motivation of the India manager.

FROM ONE COUNTRY MANAGER TO ANOTHER. Becoming the country head in India is most exhilarating and rewarding. If you enjoy new challenges; if you like to be stretched beyond your abilities; if you like to learn new things; if you like to visit remarkable places and meet interesting people; if you enjoy building a business; if you yearn to make a difference to people, to society, and to your company, there are few roles that can provide the same satisfaction as being the country head of a multinational in an emerging market. There may be a formal job description, but in reality, the job is whatever you make of it. Sure, there are boundaries and you can sometimes feel straitjacketed, but over time, if you approach the job with the right spirit and time frame, there is little that you cannot do.

Being the country head can also be brutally tough. This is not a job; it is a 24/7 mission, and it takes many years to accomplish something meaningful. It is intense. There are many incredibly frustrating moments: when you feel misunderstood and unappreciated; when you feel angry and let down by people; when you ask yourself if it's worth it. It's an extraordinary test of who you are as a person and as a leader.

To make this one of the defining experiences of your life, two things are important to recognize. One, you need the right perspective. Remember the story of the three stonecutters? A man runs into three stonecutters and asks them what they are doing. The first replies that it is obvious that he is cutting stones. The second says that he is cutting stones to build a wall. The third looks up at the sky and responds that he is helping to build a cathedral. They are all doing the same work, but the spirit and perspective they bring to it is different and so is their experience of it. It's much the same with being a country manager. You can approach it as a three-year stint and do a competent job, or you can see it as a unique opportunity to build an institution, to affect lives and society, to make a difference, and to leave a legacy. I have found it much more satisfying to bring such a sense of purpose to the role. That helped sustain me through many challenges and disappointments. It also helped me be more successful.

The second thing to recognize is that taking a long-term approach implies that this is a marathon, not a sprint. It's important to manage yourself and not burn out. Years ago, I was asked: if you cannot manage yourself, how can you manage an organization of thousands of people? Good question. Given the intensity of the role, its challenges, and its relentless nature, you have to learn to be more disciplined and manage yourself and your life. This means taking care of yourself physically, eating right, and exercising, despite the grueling hours and travel. You have to cultivate balance, taking the time for vacations, being with family, sustaining friendships, and developing a hobby. That means disconnecting and having the discipline to shut off your e-mail and phone. It's important to have people who will be honest with you and give you the feedback you need to hear. It's vital to have a good mentor whom you can turn to for wisdom. Being disciplined makes a dramatic difference to productivity and your resilience. Those elements are important if you want to achieve your full potential.[5]

THE TAKEAWAYS

- In India and China, companies have the opportunity to build multibillion-dollar businesses but have to work in a challenging environment. To do this, the country head must be an entrepreneurial general manager, not a sales head.

- The country manager role in these countries is a smaller version or microcosm of the global CEO's role. There are few roles in a company where a leader has a complete view of the company and all its products, brands, and functions. So these are ideal roles to develop the next generation of executive leadership.

- Implicit trust in the character, judgment, and competence of the country manager is of paramount importance, given the cultural and geographic distance and the many risks in India. Trust has four aspects. Integrity and honesty are obvious. A second is good judgment; many situations that arise every day require an immediate response based on sound common sense. Trust is knowing that the country manager is aligned with the global strategy and that he or she isn't pursuing a different agenda. Finally, trust is confidence in the country manager's ability to execute well and be predictable. That's why many companies put a trusted veteran in the role rather than someone who knows the market. They must resolve this compromise; the country manager must be someone who knows the market and is trusted.

- Many traits and competencies are needed for success, but five are extraordinarily good determinants of successful leaders: entrepreneurship, courage, a higher purpose, learning agility, and people skills or emotional intelligence. Assessing candidates for these qualities and developing them in the pipeline of rising leaders is vital.

4

The India Strategy and Operating Model

The trick in globalizing is to strike the delicate balance between being mindlessly global and helplessly local.

—ASHOK GANGULY, FORMER CHAIRMAN, HINDUSTAN UNILEVER

October 2010. John Flannery, president of GE India, had a big smile on his face as he left a celebration in Delhi at which CEO Jeff Immelt had congratulated GE's India team for winning a $750 million gas turbine deal—India's largest order for turbines—from Reliance Power. The main reason GE India had won against tough German and cheaper Chinese competitors was speed: the company took sixty days from bid to close. Reliance Power had been amazed; a year earlier, it would have taken GE India anywhere from nine to twelve months to put together such a complex deal. Each unit would have negotiated separately with the customer and lawyers would have taken months to wordsmith each clause.

This time around, the GE India team, operating under the "One GE" model that Immelt had unveiled a year earlier, had been empowered to close the commercial transaction from end to end, which included arranging for financing. Determined to prove the operating model's power to Reliance and to GE's headquarters, the GE India team worked 24/7 to win the contract with the full backing of the global GE network that provided technical expertise and supply chain capability. It marked the vindication of GE's new strategy and operating model for India, and signaled a reversal of fortunes for a company whose revenues had declined from $2.1 billion in 2008 to $1.6 billion in 2009.

Consider an example from another industry. By 2008, telecom giant Nokia dominated the Indian mobile handset market, with a share of nearly 70 percent. India had become Nokia's second-largest market after China. The company had executed a textbook-perfect strategy, making an early commitment to India, developing a wide range of models at different price points, investing in manufacturing and distribution reach, and building a respected brand. Then, a few unknown Indian companies like Micromax, Spice, Zen, and Karbonn started offering an unusual product. Using low-cost chipsets from a Chinese company called Mediatek, their innovation was a handset that could take two SIM cards. Customers liked these phones because they could take advantage of concessional offers from Indian telecom operators, which were then waging an all-out tariff war. One SIM card (and telephone number) stayed constant, allowing friends and family to call. Customers would swap out the second SIM card every month to take advantage of the best deal for outgoing calls. Despite frantic pleas by Nokia India for such phones, it wasn't until June 2011 that Nokia Finland finally responded by developing the dual SIM phones, C1 and C2. The consequences were catastrophic: by then, Nokia's market share had plunged to under 30 percent, while the upstarts captured almost 30 percent of the market.[1]

Why did Nokia in Finland not respond decisively to what its local team so clearly saw? How did GE change and allow its Indian operation to move quickly? The answer to both questions lies in what I call the India operating model.

Until now, multinational companies have done well in countries that resemble their home markets. They don't do as well in countries like India that are economically and culturally very different. Except for a few industries like commercial aircraft and armaments, a one-size-fits-all approach guarantees irrelevance in emerging markets. However, standardization is critical to success in a multinational company that plans to operate in many countries. Limiting product proliferation drives economy of scale, while replicating structures, procedures, and processes reduces complexity, improves control, and reduces risk.

The trick though is to get the balance between localization and standardization right. For every company like Apple that is a nonstarter in India due to its extreme standardization, there are counterexamples like Phillips that failed because they may have allowed country organizations too much freedom. Although scholars like C. K. Prahalad, Sumantra Ghoshal, and Chris Bartlett have studied the problem of how to organize global organizations, they offer few practical solutions. Because it is hard to manage both globalization and localization, many corporations default to standardization. This causes them to be uncompetitive in emerging markets including India. Next I will present some lessons from companies that have struck a better balance between the two tensions than their competitors have.

Building an Agile Operating Model

A company will operate in a unique way in one country only because the economic, business, cultural, and geographic distances from its home market are such that it has little chance of succeeding if it doesn't. Does that mean it would be willing to do things differently in Vietnam or Mozambique? Probably not; the size of the prize has to justify the cost of operating differently there.

To succeed in big markets like Japan, China, and India, companies need to be willing to find a good balance between standardization

FIGURE 4-1

Components of an agile operating model

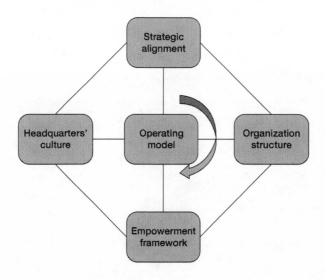

and local responsiveness. In my experience, I have found that means thinking through four issues that make up the India operating model (see figure 4-1).

1. What is the strategy that will help us win in India?

2. How do we get the whole company engaged in executing it?

3. What is the most appropriate structure to execute this strategy? What is the right empowerment framework; that is, what decisions are best made locally? What decisions must be made at headquarters? What decisions should be made jointly and what is a good process for that?

4. How does our culture at headquarters need to change to support the strategy?

Let's tackle each of them.

1. Developing the India Strategy

The first order of business is to get the entire company to develop and execute a shared strategy for India. The structure and other elements of the operating model flow from that.

Most multinational companies are matrix organizations; people are responsible for product divisions or business units, geographies, customer segments, and functions. Everyone has at least two bosses. Implementing anything requires the consensus and commitment of a broad group of people, especially the global product divisions that are often the dominant axis of the organization. Getting functions and product divisions or business units aligned around a country is often difficult, but it's powerful when there is a framework that helps make it happen. That's when things actually move very quickly, as we saw in the case of GE turbines.

In the absence of such a framework, every small thing becomes a negotiation and an act of persuasion, which is time-consuming and draining for everyone. People have to negotiate every discount and justify every hire. E-mails fly back and forth, frustration grows, and emotions rise. It's no one's fault; everyone is simply doing his or her job and operating in what he or she perceives to be in the best interests of the company, except there is no alignment around what will help the company win in India.

Developing an operating framework isn't easy, but the process must start by creating a three-year plan for India. I have seldom seen any company achieve a major transformation without senior leadership committing to a multiyear plan. Ensuring that the company draws up such a plan and getting the whole organization behind the three or four drivers of its success are the principal responsibilities of the country manager in India. With a framework and three-year operating plan that has the blessings of executive management, the bureaucracy becomes a strength. Everyone executes his or her part, which is what global companies do well.

That's how we started at Microsoft India. In August 2004, Kevin Johnson, then worldwide head of sales and marketing (now CEO of Juniper), corralled Steve Ballmer and a number of the most senior people at Microsoft's headquarters in Redmond, Washington, into a conference room with my India leadership team. We seized the opportunity to outline and discuss how to recalibrate aspirations and invest in seven growth areas in India. Because of the excitement that resulted in the room, in October 2004, Craig Mundie, then chief strategy and technology officer, and Johnson led a team of twenty-five senior Microsoft leaders on a one-week visit to India.

On day one in Delhi, we got the visitors to arrive at a common understanding of India and Microsoft's business in India, mainly through presentations and guest speakers. On days two and three, the visiting executives immersed themselves in various aspects of doing business in different parts of India. Some visited large Indian business process outsourcing companies like Infosys and Wipro in Bangalore; some spent time with small software companies in Hyderabad. Others visited big customers like Tata and Reliance in Mumbai, while the rest spent time with ministers and bureaucrats in Delhi to understand the government and policy issues. On day four, we reconvened in Delhi and shared experiences and observations. By the end of the day, Johnson and I had led the group to develop what became our first five-year strategy for India.

This investment of senior management time transformed Microsoft's trajectory in India. The resulting energy, quality of ideas, and commitment were astonishing. The budgeting process in December operationalized the plan, and Microsoft India was off to the races. We accelerated growth from 13 percent a year to over 35 percent per annum (CAGR) over the next five years. We struck partnerships with big Indian

IT firms like Infosys, transformed our relationship with the government of India, and established new businesses—Microsoft Research, Microsoft Global Services, and Microsoft IT, for instance—to leverage the talent in India. In three years, India had become the fastest-growing market in the Microsoft world, and Microsoft India was consistently rated one of the country's most respected companies.

Similar processes worked in other companies; the details vary, but all resulted in the entire company becoming committed to a multiyear plan for India. Dell's India CEO Ganesh Laxminarayan got his extended team together in 2010 and developed an aspirational plan called "3 In 3;" that is, grow from $1 billion to $3 billion in three years. He leveraged a visit by Michael Dell to get broad support and feedback, and followed up by having strategy reviews via videoconference with each leader in Austin, Texas, to create commitment and interlock. The plan, 3 In 3, has become the operating plan for Dell's units in India and is the basis of all discussions with the parent company.

At JCB India, managing director Vipin Sondhi realized that the keys to success were a manufacturing transformation and an overhaul of the dealer network. In 2006, he engaged Alan Blake, then the head of manufacturing and now JCB's CEO, in developing a plan for transforming JCB India. A team from headquarters visited world-class manufacturing plants in India, like those of Maruti Suzuki, Tata Motors, and Tata Automation, and developed a road map for manufacturing JCB products in India. A second team focused on modernizing and extending the dealer network. Despite the Great Recession of 2008 in the United States and Europe, JCB chairperson Sir Anthony Bamford insisted that the company follow through on the plans. By 2011, the result was the creation in India of the world's largest, most modern, and lowest-cost manufacturing facility for backhoe loaders and a contemporary dealer network for construction machinery.

A common set of principles guided all three approaches:

- The company must develop the strategy collaboratively between the Indian leadership team and senior leaders from headquarters drawn from various functions and divisions. It is therefore not India's strategy, which is easy to ignore, but rather the company's strategy for India. That engenders a different level of commitment at headquarters.

- There is a multiyear plan for market leadership that is refreshed every year. Most multinational companies that operate on a one-year plan end up taking a short-term view of the business in India. Investments that take more than one year to pay off—in setting up a manufacturing plant, building distribution reach, or localizing a product—are deferred. Moving to a three-year horizon is critical to unlock growth, and the company should revisit the plan as often as necessary. Bosch does that annually; JCB, given the explosive growth between 2004–2007, every quarter.

- The company develops the strategy through immersive experiences in the local market. In large companies, executives review and debate strategic plans in meeting rooms, dominated by financial numbers, PowerPoint slides, and Excel spreadsheets. Decision makers at headquarters usually ask for more and more data. However, since they lack a visceral feel for the market, the risks seem bigger and the opportunities seem smaller. The insatiable appetite for more data and evidence leads to costly delays, and eventually, the company will have to play catch-up with rivals.

  In contrast, one successful Indian entrepreneur spends a lot of time in retail shops, simply watching and listening. That, along with gut feelings, gives him the confidence to act swiftly on business opportunities without endless cycles of debate and data gathering. Global companies must ensure that their market discovery and strategic planning process in India, and other key markets, is immersive so that senior leaders develop an intuitive sense for opportunities, not just a data-driven point of view.

- The global CEO must play an active role in the process. He or she has to provide the mandate for developing a strategy in the first place, must be engaged in reviews with the executive management team, and must help resolve contentious issues, such as how additional investments in India will be funded, who has the final say on pricing and hiring in India, whether the company must develop market-specific products, and under what brands the new products should be sold. It is imperative that the CEO hold the executive leadership accountable for the results in India, not just the leader to whom India reports organizationally.

THE THREE HORIZONS. Talking about an India strategy across industries and companies is difficult, but a few themes are evident. One theme is that the greater the dependence on government, the less attractive the business. All the evidence suggests that industries dependent on state policy, government regulations, and access to public resources, like infrastructure, mining, and natural resources, find tough going in India. In fact, given the regulatory problems and corruption, multinational companies find it nearly impossible to enter and succeed in these industries. By contrast, sectors at an arm's length from government, like banking, IT, pharmaceuticals, and consumer goods, flourish even when the state may be ineffective.

A second theme is that a company needs to straddle the pyramid to be successful in India. It has to sell global products at global prices to the affluent, innovate to find success in the middle market, and engage with the bottom of the pyramid through social enterprises, shared value initiatives, and public-private partnership with the government. The India opportunity in most industries is not the small global segment at the top, but the big middle market. This is as true for industrial products as it is for consumer goods. For instance, in India's commercial vehicles market, sales in the premium segment are around one thousand trucks a year, while the market volume is around three hundred thousand trucks. To make a mark in India, companies can start at the top, but they must break into the difficult middle market, developing a localized business model that allows them to be profitable at low price points.

Cracking the middle market takes time. Companies have to experiment, tweaking products, pricing, and go-to-market approaches to build a low-cost business model. It takes iteration and debate over what elements of the global model they should modify. Moreover, India is not one market; it is much more a region like Europe. Companies have to develop granular strategies covering segments, products, cities, and channels. That takes time and tenacity. Tata Cummins took six years to achieve a profitable business model and three more years to pay off all accumulated losses. The joint venture now generates a healthy chunk of Cummins's global profits.

Figuring out the approach to the top, middle, and bottom of the pyramid in India conceptually mirrors McKinsey's three horizons growth model.[2] Horizon one, the here-and-now priority, entails replicating the global business model in India, while horizon two involves figuring out a successful model for the middle market, which will take significant investment and energy. Horizon three contains ideas for long-term profitable growth; these are usually small experiments, research, and investments in social enterprises and start-ups. At Hindustan Unilever (HUL), a horizon-one priority would be to sell more Dove soap or Surf detergent to upper-middle-class homes. Horizon two might be scaling HUL's rural distribution system through women's self-help groups. The Pureit water filter, a fundamentally new business for Unilever, is a horizon-three opportunity.

Nitin Paranjpe, head of HUL, articulated a third theme. While HUL is well established in India, the market is intensely competitive and its leadership is under attack by lots of hungry competitors. What matters most for HUL is to be at the head of major market trends and disruptions. "What we need to ensure is that we position ourselves ahead of trends, so they provide a tailwind and not a headwind," explains Paranjpe. Planning at HUL, stemming I suspect from its near-death experience with low-cost detergent manufacturer Nirma two decades ago, is driven by the identification of the most important trends. Some recent trends that HUL is concerned with are sustainability, the rise of organized retail. The strategy process ensures a robust point of view on each trend, and the country manager must develop a plan to benefit from them. Agility is about spotting these trends early; it's not about running after them later on. Having a dominant market share in the emerging trend is critical. For new entrants, especially those up against entrenched incumbents, it is critical to embrace new trends ahead of the incumbent; that's their only chance of getting into the game.

Another strategic decision is on the use of joint ventures and acquisitions to gain scale. These are important ways of building critical mass and scale in a new market like India. Making joint ventures work is challenging, but companies like Cummins, Volvo, Suzuki, Honda, and GE have been successful in doing so. Acquisitions too have risks and are often value destructive, but can speed up growth, as Schneider Electric, DHL, and Abbott Laboratories have done in India. (In chapter 6, I will discuss the use of JVs and acquisitions in greater depth.)

Finally, growth in markets like India often occurs in unpredictable spurts, rather than in a continuous fashion (see figure 4-2). Few people anticipated how the economy would lift off in 2004–2005; fewer anticipated the rapid deceleration in 2011. A company needs to position itself well, and when the spurt starts, give it everything it has and ride the tiger. This is not the time to hold back or limit investments or support. Later in this chapter, I will describe how JCB seized the moment. Another company might have celebrated 40 percent growth and been satisfied. But what if there is an opportunity to be growing at 100 percent? It's important to floor it. Most races are won in the turns; anyone can floor it on the straights. So it was at JCB, where the whole company exerted itself to push the limits in India. The results were amazing.

FIGURE 4-2

Growth in India happens in spurts followed by periods of slowdown (compared with China)

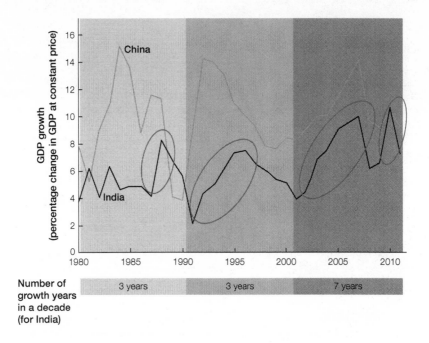

Source: International Monetary Fund, World Economic Outlook Database, April 2012.

2. Keeping the Structure Simple and Accountable

As I conducted my research, I discovered that any discussion about organizational structures touched a nerve in nearly every company I visited. In most multinationals, there are global divisions and functional organizations in each region. So the HR, finance, and legal departments in India report to their global counterparts functionally, as do the different business units. This is often taken to an extreme, where different parts of finance—tax, treasury, and accounting, for instance—report separately to different heads. In HR, training, compensation, and benefits also report globally, rather than to the India HR head. The strong country organizations of the 1960s, led by powerful managers who ran their operations with a lot of freedom, have given way to stronger global product divisions and global functions.

There are several reasons for this approach, but the fact is that in many companies, the dominant axis is the business unit or product division; those businesses are global and their presidents are accountable for financial results. They naturally want control and linkages with their businesses in every country. In theory, these linkages are important for understanding local opportunities, developing local talent and capability, and supporting the local business with deep expertise, investments, and resources. It's a sensible way to run a global business.

Unsurprisingly, most country managers hate matrixed organizations with dual reporting relationships. This is not an issue of control or ego; the problem is that since India contributes only 1 percent of global revenues, it gets 1 percent of the attention of the senior people at headquarters and even less of the investment. They can meet global targets without paying much attention to their business in India, which will stay stuck in the midway trap that I described in chapter 2. Dual reporting often leads to confusion, turf battles, unclear accountability, and enormous amounts of time spent in negotiating simple decisions.

There is a high risk of losing flexibility and speed, especially in geographies where the confusion is exacerbated by language, time zone, cultural, and hierarchical barriers.

Senior leaders in multinational companies are ambivalent about creating straight-line in-country reporting and accountability for all businesses, pointing out that there is no ideal structure. Whichever axis a company organizes around—product, geography, or segment—it has no choice but to make the other two axes work. In their seminal book *Managing Across Borders: The Transnational Solution 2002*, Sumantra Ghoshal and Chris Bartlett argue that matrix organizations are a frame of mind rather than a structure.[3] Companies need general managers with matrices in their minds.

However, creating the culture that supports matrix management is hard. A fascinating case study by IIM Bangalore lays out the challenges of Bosch in India as it moved from a geographical to a matrix organization where global product groups dominate.[4] The new organization created fragmentation, conflict, and other challenges, while pursuing opportunities and managing across businesses in India. For instance, the authors write:

> Previously, Bosch in India was one group. There was a country head and all issues pertaining to India were resolved efficiently. With multiple reporting within India … there are conflicts and, often, long delays in resolving simple issues. Since production divisions and sales divisions are different, they now fight over transfer prices … This often leads to a blame game. A lot of time is spent on conflict resolution. The head of a division in India has to report to the managing director of Bosch India for disciplinary (i.e., administrative) purposes and to a person in the Asia region for his targets. Within the division, there are three verticals: Sales, engineering, and manufacturing. The head of engineering reports to the head of the division for disciplinary purposes but to

a different person in Asia for targets. The same holds for the head of manufacturing. Each also has a functional reporting relationship with a third person, who may be located in another geography. Earlier, investment decisions were made in India. Now that people in Germany drive these divisions, some of these investments may be unsuitable for the Indian context. For instance, they may want an investment in an automated assembly line based on the European context even if in the Indian context, manual assembly may be more suitable.

In the past, the country head might see potential in the market that the business group did not see. The global group will have global priorities and may neglect India in preference to another geography. An Indian client may develop an engine and want us to develop a component but we might not be able to take it up, as it may not get the approval of the global products group. In the past, we developed things like a hand-held marble cutter, which has a market only in India. We might not be able to do that now. There is less discretion in maintaining practices unique to the Indian context. For example, taking high-performing dealers on a trip was possible with local approval. Since this is not the practice in other countries, it is difficult to get approval from the global products group, which is a norm in Indian industry. Executives in India also feel that the culture and low maturity of managers makes the matrix harder to work in India. Multiple reporting relationships give scope for personalities to come into play. Strong assertive personalities dominate weak and submissive ones.[5]

The dual reporting structure in many companies can be made to work, but it requires mature leaders, both at headquarters and in the regions, who are able to keep the best interests of the company ahead of their functional or divisional interests. Imprinting the matrix in the

mind of managers and establishing processes for making dual reporting work—for instance, joint performance appraisals—take thought
and effort, and many companies haven't done what it takes. The global
leaders of divisions and functions must have country-specific goals for
major countries like India, so they are forced to engage with it.

Even so, the matrix structure is a compromise. I am skeptical,
particularly when companies want to grow faster than the industry.
Companies that lack scale in India need to bite the bullet as GE has
finally done. It is better to move to a simple structure where all the
functions and businesses needed to execute the business plan report
to a country head who becomes the point of accountability. Then the
country manager's job is to ensure coordination and alignment with
global functions, segments, and product divisions, and to make the
matrix tick, while the three-year plan becomes the vehicle for creating
alignment. If the country manager is a senior executive whom headquarters trusts, this will not pose a big risk.

The logic is simple: India is 1 percent of the business for a global
president in New York; it is 100 percent of the business for the country
manager in Delhi. Focus, proximity to the market, and connecting
every day with local people result in commitment, intensity, and
insight, which are hard to get otherwise. That's a major factor in the
success of Cummins, JCB, Nestlé, Schneider Electric, and, since 2010,
GE India. GE India is a classic instance where putting all the responsibility and accountability under a strong, senior, and trusted country
president with the authority to make most operating decisions per-
taining to commercial terms, hiring, and investments up to $250 mil-
lion (over 3–5 years) has transformed the company's performance.
After stagnation for much of the last decade and decline in revenues
in some years, GE India is again growing at nearly 50 percent annually. Conversely, a radiating organizational structure, where every
leader reports to someone different outside India, is affecting the performance of companies like Caterpillar and Salesforce.

Sure, there are challenges with making the country the dominant axis. Some local leaders in India may experience a loss of autonomy; they will have a boss in the same country far more engaged with their business than a boss in Singapore or Paris. There may also be loss of prestige. "They were ministers in the federal government of GE, and now they're ministers in the state government of Flannery," points out an observer about the changes at GE. Global business heads will have concerns, too; someone else will be making strategic, investment, and operational decisions about their businesses in India. First China, now India; where will it all end?

Country managers, too, must learn to deal with the stresses of operating in such models. For instance, when I led Cummins in India, we deviated from the global go-to-market model in our power-generation business. Cummins designs, assembles, and distributes or sells generator sets. In India, we decided to strike strategic partnerships with three generator set manufacturers. They would make and sell the sets but based on a standardized design, using key components that Cummins supplied and with Cummins's dealer network providing after-sales service. This was hugely successful because it combined scale economies and standardization with the entrepreneurial flair of local businesspersons. We came to this decision to deviate not unilaterally, but collaboratively with the global business head and agreed to approach it as an experiment. There were other times when we made more unilateral decisions about pricing, product features, or investing in a business that was growing locally but faced an investment and headcount freeze globally. Those were the right decisions for India, but contentious, and the CEO had to arbitrate. This tension, when it plays out constructively and collaboratively between senior leaders, makes the model successful.

To accelerate growth in India dramatically, the country organization must be powerful. However, once India is a significant part of the global business, it may make sense to go back to the traditional model. When the organization and its leaders are mature, people and talent flows are strong, and it becomes important to scale innovations and capabilities in India to other markets, the pendulum may have to swing toward more integration rather than geographic focus. That's what Unilever is trying to do under current CEO Paul Polman and perhaps why GE in China is still aligned globally.

THE UNDIVIDED INDIA ORGANIZATION. India and China are unique in that multinational companies have multiple back-end operations in those countries, including IT, engineering, and global procurement. Each unit is independent, with a strong leader reporting to a global head. These units must have tight operational linkages with their functions at headquarters, but it's important that the leaders of these units administratively report to the local country manager.

The country manager must formally be the first among equals and play the role of unifier across these disparate units, so the public face or image is of one company, recruiting on college campuses is coordinated, and there are opportunities for employees to move across these units instead of being confined to their own silo. There must be a shared services model for HR, finance, and public relations and communications across all these units. There is often an opportunity to leverage the functional and technical expertise in these units to help customers. Microsoft was successful at leveraging expertise at its India Development Center, Microsoft IT, and Global Services Center to help customers get the most out of their IT investments. That became a powerful differentiator.

It's important to formalize a One GE, One Microsoft, or One IBM model and not leave it to people or chance. The country head should lead the India executive team, and a charter should describe what the team should attempt to accomplish. The global leader, the country head, and the country HR leader should do the hiring and performance appraisals. Surprisingly, few companies have actually made the effort to formalize such a governance model, resulting in compliance problems, people issues, suboptimal business performance, a fragmented public image, and an unsatisfactory experience for employees who yearn to be part of something bigger.

Regional reporting is losing its importance in the next phase of globalization. An Asian regional headquarters that embraces developed markets like Japan, South Korea, and Australia; emerging giants China and India; and small markets like Cambodia and Vietnam makes limited sense. Establishing the regional headquarters in pristine and orderly Singapore, staffed by expatriate managers, can result in another layer of bureaucracy that slows things down.

China, India, Brazil, and some other emerging markets are distinct, with many similarities. Grouping them together makes more sense than the traditional time zone regions of EMEA (Europe, Middle East, and Africa), LATAM (Latin America), and APAC (Asia Pacific). It also allows companies to appoint leaders who are knowledgeable about emerging markets and have built businesses in one of them to take responsibility for all emerging markets. Honeywell's Tedjarati oversees all high-growth markets and operates out of China with a miniscule staff, for instance.

Business leaders like Jaspal Bindra, a board member at Standard Chartered Bank, point out that:

> Having a corps of people who know India and other major emerging markets is a benefit that is only recently begun to be appreciated. They have the context to say, "I can appreciate this," "I understand that," or "That doesn't sound right." It allows us to have a more confident approach to the market with a balanced approach to risk. Building such an institutional understanding of key geographies at HQ is critical. Putting an executive in charge who has only limited experience in and of emerging markets makes little sense.

One recent trend is to have global roles in India. For instance, Honeywell's global head of manufacturing and engineering and Dell's global head of services operate out of Bangalore. Cummins India's chairperson is the global head of the components business; Reckitt Benckiser India has responsibility for Southeast Asia; and at Schneider Electric, the CEO and a third of the leadership team have moved to Hong Kong to be closer to Asia. Such shifts in the flow of people promote greater understanding and integration. It's easier to attract talented executives when they don't have to leave India to grow. The CEO sleeps easy at night knowing there are people sensing problems and opportunities that the system might take a long time to detect. This is part of the multinational company's evolution from the hub-and-spoke model to having a small headquarters and multiple hubs with national and global missions.

3. The Company Way: Empowerment with Accountability

The East India Company, established in 1600 AD, was the first modern multinational, a pioneer of many governance systems and approaches. From a small headquarters building, a tiny staff administered a sprawling global empire. A few thousand Englishmen with a median age of thirty managed to rule a nation of 250 million people in India. Communications were usually dispatches sent by horse and ship; a response to a question would take a minimum of six months. Micromanagement, the way we know it, was impossible.

How did the company men do it?[6] The answer lies in trust-based governance and accountability. London refined a process to hire prodigiously gifted, entrepreneurial, frequently aristocratic young men, ensured they had a fine education at the company's college in Haileybury, and sent them to India with a sense of mission. The governor-general and district collectors were trusted employees who enjoyed tremendous responsibility and freedom.

Modern multinationals would do well to emulate some (though not all) of the East India Company's practices. The crux is to move from control to trust with accountability. Many companies make decisions of very modest consequence outside India. As several country managers admitted to me, "We can't buy even a pencil without HQ approval. Pricing discounts, hiring three people, investing $10,000, leasing a building, negotiating hotel tariffs … every decision requires the approval of someone outside India." It's demotivating. In addition, every little decision involves marketing, wasting time, and distracting people from serving customers and creating value. Holding leaders accountable for performance becomes harder; after all, someone else made the decisions. Performance suffers.

As countries grow in size and importance, decision rights are seldom recalibrated. Regional headquarters continue to treat India like Vietnam. This is particularly true if there is a large staff; the armies of bright people need work, so questioning even modest decisions becomes part of the standard operating routine. A culture of distrust also plays a role; if you don't understand these markets and don't have a leadership team you trust, micromanagement will be necessary.

The more optimal way of balancing empowerment with good governance is to move from control to accountability. You do that by appointing a country manager in India whose ethics, judgment, and alignment you trust, as I described in chapter 3. Then you create a new empowerment framework from a clean sheet of paper by asking not what decisions India can make, but rather what decisions India can't unilaterally make. The exception-based approach is important to unlock entrepreneurship. At McDonald's, which works with fiercely independent franchisees, the agreement covers just a few areas where franchisees cannot unilaterally make decisions; they have total freedom in everything else. That's how McDonald's unlocks entrepreneurship.

I vividly recollect my conversations with J. S. Shin, the president of Samsung Electronics India. He struggled to comprehend the question about empowerment. Finally, he said: "For some decisions, such as building a new factory, I must consult my colleagues in South Korea. Otherwise, 99 percent of the decisions are taken in Delhi." Samsung is able to operate like that because Shin is a thirty-year company veteran who previously headed global marketing for the digital appliances division. With Samsung growing in India at over 50 percent a year on a base of $5 billion, it isn't possible to micromanage the business from Seoul. Similarly, no one manages GE India's Flannery or his head count; he doesn't have to ask for permission if he needs to hire fifty salespeople. He has a kitty of $250 million to invest in market opportunities at his discretion.

Even Walmart, a company associated with strong centralization in Bentonville, Arkansas, has a principle of delegating authority closest to the customer to allow the greatest flexibility and speed of response. It does this using an approach called Freedom within a Box, which maximizes a country's or a store's decision-making authority and flexibility. The idea is simply to maximize the number of decisions that the local team can make and to have a framework to work out how the rest are decided. In fact, joint ventures and listed subsidiaries are helpful in localizing a business because joint-venture agreements require that its management team and board of directors make most of the operating decisions locally.

4. Creating a Supportive Culture at Headquarters

One company that I grew to admire while writing this book is JCB, the plucky construction equipment maker from England's Midlands. Despite the deindustrialization of the United Kingdom, the company is thriving, with a manufacturing base in the heart of the country. It has decisively beaten Goliaths like Caterpillar and Komatsu in India and gained global market share in its industry. On the face of it, the reasons are simple. The controlling family member, Sir Anthony Bamford, took a long-term view of the market and made early investments in getting the right product, localizing it, and establishing a low-cost supply chain and a superb dealer network. When the market took off after 2005, JCB was ready to seize the opportunity, and business exploded. A long-term view of the market was rewarded by good luck. Or was it really so simple?

Among other things, JCB's corporate culture may have played a key role. To illustrate this point, here are some snippets from my conversation with Sir Anthony Bamford.

Reflecting on JCB's great success in India, Sir Anthony says:

Luck played a big role in our success. I liked India. I traveled through India as a young man with long hair and just loved it. I always had a high opinion of Indian managers and engineers. I decided we must be there even though my father (founder JC Bamford) disagreed strongly. Obviously I had no idea that India would grow in this way though … you couldn't tell it was going to happen in that way.

On his basic philosophy:

I hated companies that would try to sell in India what they could no longer sell here and send over their old tooling. I wanted India to always have the best of everything. Not old products or old machines. My fondest desire is for the best products to come out of our Indian factories with the best quality and cost … we very much believe in running the business with Indians … we can't run India from here, so we put in place the best management team we could find. We have very few expats except where technical expertise is critical. This helped us when India started to grow rapidly.

On the relationship between HQ and India:

I am very opposed to hierarchy and a class system ... I think it is wrong. I don't like us versus them. I hated imperialism of any sort and took extra precautions to beat it out. We work hard on the culture of how we at HQ work with India. I told our team here (in HQ), "Put India in front not behind ... we exist to help India be successful." If I see a manager who isn't handling things very well (i.e., being unhelpful to India), I will do something about it. I would do the same with any of our Indian managers ... I message down what is appropriate by demonstration and reinforcement. We have tried to encourage a culture that is eager to share and hungry to learn and with large numbers of people going back and forth.

On how JCB has benefited from its operations in India:

You give an idea to India and it comes back even better. We have learned more from India than we have taught India. We have our best dealer body in the world in India and it has forced us to evolve our franchise discipline, it has changed how we approach dealers and we can apply this in other parts of the world. We ensured our Indian colleagues understood how much we learn from them ... it's critical to make this learning a two-way not one-way process. India is now a very significant part of our business so by right they have a place at the top table ... In all our groupwide communication I make sure people understand how important India is to JCB. In the darkest time in 2009–2010, I made no bones about the fact that India was paying our wages.

Finally, thoughts on the future of India:

Some of my colleagues from British industry still feel it's risky going to India because they had a bad experience twenty years ago ... Look, we have had many problems on the way but we always took a long-term view and things worked out very well. It was always start-stop rather than any real problems. Honestly I can't see anything that would stop me from investing in India. India is a frustrating place, always five steps forward and two or three steps back but always upwards.

Like proud parents, the chairman, CEO, and executive team at JCB are keen to see the Indian company grow into a capable adult surpassing the parent. They see the role of headquarters as supporting and assisting the team, they encourage collaboration and learning, and they discourage talking down to the Indian subsidiary. Simplicity and urgency are two key themes the family emphasizes. In addition to a consistent long-term view of the business, there is humility and empathy.

Contrast this with the culture of many multinational companies. The task of building leadership is usually delegated to the head of international sales. All countries are treated the same, irrespective of opportunity, and senior leaders have little understanding of India. There's a clear us-versus-them mentality, with headquarters staff either telling the subsidiaries what to do or sitting in judgment on them, but seldom lending a helping hand. In particular, there are middle managers in functions like finance, legal, taxation, real estate, heath, safety, and environment mandated to avoid risk. They use their power to thwart rather than to facilitate business and make things happen. Country managers in India have many stories to recount. Time to transfer a real estate lease from one division to another? One year. Time to approve the purchase of a piece of land after the global CEO has given permission to proceed? One year. Time for headquarters to approve a contract after two CEOs have shaken hands on a deal? Three months. Time to hire a director-level person? Three months, because of the travel schedules of the people outside India who need to interview the candidate. During one of our conversations, Walmart's Scott Price remarked that companies that were stovepipes—that is, they had strong silos and fiefs, had the largest headquarters, the strongest staff functions, and were the most centralized and inward looking—and faced the greatest challenge in markets different from their home country. I found this to be empirically accurate.

Culture trumps strategy when it comes to globalization. Executives of multinational companies must shape the cultures of their companies through personal example and reinforcement of behaviors. In particular, they should promote significant flows of people back and forth between headquarters and key geographies for projects and assignments of less than a year. Those are easier to accomplish without being tangled up in global levels, compensation, family-relocation policies, and so on. They must keep headquarters lean and promote a culture of simplicity, with fewer of everything: fewer meetings, metrics, reviews, PowerPoint slides, and executive visits.

The role of the corporate center must be reshaped, too. That doesn't mean turning over the keys of the kingdom to the local team. The role of the center, beyond governance, lies in ensuring that the power of the global network is leveraged to win in every market. It must help transfer global expertise, best practices, talent, and products to India in support of a locally relevant plan. Conversely, it must leverage Indian talent and expertise, locally developed products, and Indian suppliers to win in other emerging markets.

THE TAKEAWAYS

- To succeed in dynamic markets with large opportunity, companies need to modify their operating models so that there is a better balance between local responsiveness and global standardization. The ability to respond quickly to customer opportunities, market shifts, and competitors' moves is important.

- Four things enable speed in a sprawling company:

1. Getting everyone—functions, product units, and customer segments—aligned and accountable for executing a multiyear plan for transformational growth in India. The responsibility lies largely between the country manager and the global CEO. Once such agreement exists, even bureaucratic companies can execute well.

2. The governance model has to move from control to trust with accountability. It should be a conscious endeavor to maximize the number of decisions within the country and have explicit agreement on what few decisions need consultation or approval.

3. Although it may be controversial, create an in-country organizational structure where everyone who is responsible for driving growth and market share reports into the country manager. Reporting locally to a senior manager with bottom-line accountability for the India business facilitates agility, ownership, and accountability.

4. Culture plays an important role. Simplicity, humility, openness, a lean headquarters, and two-way flows of people are critical to building a culture that supports emerging markets.

5

Growing Leaders

FROM LIP SERVICE TO RESULTS

The shortage of talent is the single largest issue that can affect our
growth in India.

—JOHN FLANNERY, PRESIDENT, GE INDIA

If the right country manager is the biggest determinant of success in
India, building a strong team and organization is, by far, the biggest
imperative for a country leader. In addition to delivering results
locally, a capable organization earns the confidence of the global
headquarters, ensures its commitment, and sets off a spiral of success.
The converse is equally true, and companies can fall back into the
midway trap if they fail to build capable country organizations.

In India, building an engine that pumps out talent is tough. Despite
a young population and India's vaunted education system, shortages of
every kind of talent and skill are evident in the country. A PwC survey
in 2011 showed just how critical talented people are: 41 percent of CEOs
surveyed said that they canceled or delayed a key strategic initiative,
and 39 percent said that they were unable to meet growth projections
because of a shortage of people or because the costs of hiring people
soared more than expected.[1]

The talent shortage shows up in the difficulty that companies face in retaining talent. A mobile workforce with high aspirations and low maturity has driven attrition rates in India into the high double-digits. Companies must hire even as they bleed people and compensation shoots up by between 10 percent and 15 percent every year. There's a shortage of middle managers, especially people managers who can develop frontline workers, as well as managers with expertise in functions such as product engineering, supply chain management, and project management.

Nearly every company, Indian and multinational, faces a succession challenge. There's a steep drop in leadership capability between the CEO and the next level, and an even more alarming drop one more level down. With companies growing at 20 percent to 30 percent every year, jobs outgrow incumbents, leading to the chant: "Will X grow into the job or is it time to make a change?" Sadly, there often isn't a stronger candidate.

Although talent ought to be high on CEOs' agendas, and they should be investing heavily to grow people, the reality is very different. Many companies are paying little more than lip service to the issue. Every CEO can point to the company's talent review process and leadership development programs, but in India investments in leadership development, training, and building capability are anemic. The median spending on learning and development per employee is $125 a year, rising to $300 in the top quartile. Investments in people across India Inc. are only 1.6 percent of the costs of wages—half that of the United States. Given the realities, I would have expected it to be the opposite.[2]

Companies rely disproportionately on external hires, so everyone chases the same talent. HR managers continue to be overwhelmingly focused on recruitment and retention. A 2012 Indicus–*Business Today* survey of the best companies to work for is quite telling.[3] In a bid to attract and retain employees, companies are disproportionately focused on compensation, benefits, and a work experience that includes everything from Thai foot massages to wine tastings. There's scarcely a mention of investing in building capabilities or innovative approaches to growing leaders from within. The talent crisis will likely get worse, severely limiting companies' abilities to grow faster than the industry average.

There are many reasons for this. Companies in India are on a hiring treadmill. When you have a business growing at 20 percent and attrition of 15 percent, a company is essentially hiring a third of its workforce every year. The challenges of screening, hiring, and assimilating so many people are extraordinary. Add on the pressure of delivering quarterly results, and it's almost impossible to focus on the talent agenda.

Talent development isn't a priority for headquarters either. Most multinational companies focus on succession, so it's hardly surprising that their Indian subsidiaries aren't very different. Several rely on expats, while others have a systematic bias toward filling senior roles from outside. That creates a revolving door of leaders, a mixed-up culture, and low employee commitment.

Creating a leadership engine and developing new capabilities take between five and ten years. If the country leadership team turns over every three years, and they can do well just by meeting budgets, there is no chance of building a world-class organization. In addition, building capabilities and growing leaders cost money; people have to be sent to work on projects in other parts of the world and expatriate managers may have to be flown in. If there are no budgets or head count for such things, it is hard to make progress.

Bridging the Talent Gap

Despite these factors, some companies have been able to get off the treadmill. Hindustan Unilever, for example, has earned a reputation for developing talent, alongside familiar champions such as GE and P&G in India. The sidebar "License to Lead" vividly portrays HUL's obsession for growing talent that is a striking contrast to the tick-the-box approach in many companies.[4]

License to Lead: Hindustan Unilever's Incredible Talent Grooming Machinery

Hindustan Unilever's (HUL) office in Andheri, Mumbai, lies an hour away from the legendary Wankhede Stadium, where legions of cricket fans throng to witness their cricketing gods clash in the India Premier League. Inside HUL, though, it is the Talent Super League (TSL) that's getting everyone charged up. The contenders for the TSL crowns aren't brand managers with stellar records for belting competitors out of the park or knocking down rival P&G wickets in the marketplace. The leaders of HUL compete for a different kind of award: best mentor. Interestingly, it's the mentees who decide the mentors' fates, by rating them on their performance as coaches. The high-scoring mentors are congratulated by HUL managing director Nitin Paranjpe on the famous "street" at the center of the sprawling new HUL campus, cheered on by hundreds of Leverites from the galleries. Working behind the scenes, executive director of HR, Leena Nair, and her spirited team make sure that HUL talent machinery churns out winners consistently. And for those keeping score on the number of CEOs have come out of HUL's ranks, at last count, more than four hundred CEOs (including from within Unilever) had HUL work experience on their resumes. And that's not all—there are more than two hundred HUL managers working for Unilever around the world. Even with that kind of track record, Nair's team is preparing to take the game a notch higher. Inside the HUL campus, they have unveiled a secret weapon to keep the edge on the famed Lever talent pipeline: their very own Crotonville. "Fifty Weeks of Training"—a sign at the gate of the newly inaugurated learning center makes the intention and goals clear. In plush training rooms, the displays spell out the fifty-week training programs and the components of the company's "blended learning approach": one lists online academies, another has motivating mantras like "Seek and you shall find" and Get Abstract, a learning module.

Companies often talk about people being their most important assets but this doesn't reflect in their day-to-day functioning. At HUL, learning is built into jobs. 70:20:10 is the basic tenet around which the company's training and development program is built. Simply put: 70 percent of training happens on the job, 20 percent by coaching and mentoring, and the remaining 10 percent through e-learning and classroom training. Since on-the-job training is the largest component of training, the HR department facilitates the career management of 16,000 employees (including 1,500 managers) in a way that offers new and challenging assignments and new learning opportunities. "It's a Herculean task, given that executives move on to new jobs every three to four years," acknowledges Nair.

The training for new management recruits starts from day one. New hires are put through a 15–18-month cross-functional training program that includes international exposure and three months of independent responsibility, known as subordinate charge. At the heart of the HUL training program is the Individual Development Program, a customized training program for a large number of employees. Employees are evaluated for their training needs—functional as well as leadership skills—every two years. For functional skills, the personal-skill profile of every employee is matched against the skill profile for his job to identify the gaps. The 1,500 managers go through a 360-degree evaluation where 18–20 people provide input on their leadership. An individual development program is then created, recommending classroom training and e-learning courses that will help close those gaps. On average, every manager ends up taking five e-learning courses, two classroom sessions (one functional, one leadership), and four sessions by external leaders. With more than 40,000 e-learning courses a year, HUL is the largest consumer of e-learning in all of Unilever. Classroom training adds another 2,000-plus hours toward skill development of employees.

Experts agree that corporate training programs deliver results when they are well-matched to the needs of the business. Every three years at HUL, the top 30–40 leaders undertake a vision exercise that draws up the company's ambition and sets top lines, bottom lines, market shares, targets, etc. A talent and organization plan is prepared alongside the vision document to get a fix on the present and future talent and skill needs of the organization. For example, during the last vision exercise, one of the focus areas identified was the need for better digital marketing skills. HUL hired partners, developed e-learning modules, and called in digital experts to shore up the digital skills of its marketers and, yes, every marketer had a digital skill program in his development program.

The true differentiator of HUL's training lies in its mentoring program. "A lot of organizations have training programs, but what makes ours special is the commitment of leaders to build the next generation of leaders. It's a strong part of our legacy," explains Nair. In the fifty weeks of training, more than half the programs are run by HUL's own leaders, who share their experiences with juniors. At any point in time, 300–500 managers are being mentored over and above their immediate bosses in a mentoring program. While the immediate boss is the mentor, every new recruit, new promotee, or high-potential candidate has an additional mentor. Moreover, the boss can't take mentoring lightly. Every year employees fill in a global people survey, which has 10–12 questions about the immediate boss. While the best mentors are lauded in the talent super league, the ones who lag are taken off the mentoring program for a year. For the senior leaders there's reverse mentoring as well. CEO Nitin Paranjpe, Pradeep Banerjee, executive director of supply chain, and Nair are being mentored in digital savviness. "I wasn't on Facebook, Twitter, and LinkedIn until about nine months ago. Now a young brand manager teaches me how the world is changing," says Nair. With the business landscape changing drastically in the last decade or so, an important part of development is getting leaders from outside to share their ideas, insights, and experiences with HUL managers. A program called Sip And Share has CEOs like Future Group's Kishore Biyani, Walmart's Raj Jain, and HCL's Vineet Nayar come to HUL's campus and talk about their experiences.

In the HUL universe, the shining stars are the "Listers"—managers on a fast-track career path and they constitute 15 percent of the 1,500 top-managerial talent, out of 5,000 people overall in supervisory/managerial roles. The eight members of the HUL management committee decide how the Listers will be rotated in the system, and what challenging assignments will they undertake. But even the Lister list is reviewed every year, so if the person does not perform for three years, the list is challenged. This leaves no room for doubt that within this global giant exists a league of extraordinary leaders.

Note: adapted from *License to Lead*, by Vinod Mahanta, in *Economic Times*, April 20, 2012.

The world does not need another book or even a chapter that shows how to build a talent engine or grow leaders; shelves sag with such books and Amazon has seventy-seven thousand books on leadership and twenty-two thousand on talent. I'd like to focus on answering one central issue: how do CEOs of multinational companies build a capable country-level organization in India or any other developing country?

First of all, companies have to get serious about growing leaders. Many companies point to the wonderful things they do to develop leaders, but when the time comes to fill key roles, they find they have no internal talent. Successors who are "ready now," it often turns out, aren't quite ripe to take over, so companies have to rely on search firms. The problem is that when you go outside the company, the person you hire doesn't fit into the culture more than half the time. The interview is a notoriously weak process; it's a conversation between two liars, goes the joke. Even reference checks don't help. The cost of failure is large. Besides, young leaders become demotivated when they see juicy roles repeatedly going to outsiders. Above all, the company's culture becomes a weird mishmash of the values that various leaders brought with them. Why do I say this? Because, at one stage, I made the mistake of relying almost entirely on external hires. Our business was growing at between 35 percent and 45 percent a year, jobs were growing faster than incumbents were, and I hesitated to bet on the devils I knew, preferring the ones I didn't. Big mistake!

The journey toward creating a leadership engine begins with two simple but vital rules. Without them, leadership development will never be taken seriously.

Rule One: Growing leaders is a necessary condition for a promotion. Companies that don't build a talent engine don't hold senior leaders accountable for growing leaders; what matters are financial results. At GE India and Hindustan Unilever, half the senior management's bonus is driven by organizational outcomes. The number of leaders developed is a fundamental criterion for advancement.

Rule Two: 70 percent of management roles must be filled from within. Every exception will require the approval of the country manager.

Next, identify people with fire, passion, courage, and entrepreneurial flair, and give them big jobs and big challenges—bigger than they are ready for. You must then do everything possible to help them succeed. And you must do this repeatedly. These big jobs and big challenges become crucibles for leadership development and provide the context for mentoring, coaching, and classroom learning. The stresses of trying to survive and excel create leaders.

I say this from personal experience. In 1988, when I was twenty-five years old, I was given the opportunity to be a shop-floor supervisor in a Cummins plant in Indiana that was heading for closure and had a tough industrial relations record. I was thirty when I became the general manager of a group of underperforming businesses, and my mandate was to fix, sell, or close them. At thirty-two, I found myself the managing director of a troubled joint venture between Cummins and Tata Motors in India. At thirty-five, I was given the responsibility for all of Cummins's businesses in India and appointed chairperson of the publicly listed Cummins India.

I was underprepared for each of these roles, which were bigger than my ability at that time. However, the leaders at Cummins put young managers with potential through progressively bigger challenges. They had the courage to take the risks of doing so. Few of us let the company down, working harder and smarter to justify the faith they had placed in us. What we lacked in maturity and experience we made up in effort and our willingness to learn. Cummins's entire global leadership has come up the same way, including my former colleague and peer, Tom Linebarger, currently the company's chairman and CEO. The credit for much of my professional success goes to the remarkable leaders of Cummins at that time.

A related practice is to link strategy and leadership development. In most companies, these are disconnected processes. By contrast, Indian CEOs who have an outstanding record of grooming CEOs, such as Ashok Ganguly of Hindustan Unilever and K. V. Kamath of ICICI Bank, see strategy and leadership development as inextricably intertwined. The companies' major strategic initiatives are, by design, led by next-generation leaders and staffed by rising stars. They give them tough missions, such as launching a new business or turning around a business unit. Those become crucibles for leadership development, in which mentoring, coaching, executive education, and strategy development are anchored. The CEO and senior leaders engage deeply with these teams, and they assess and mentor several generations of leaders. Close observation enables precise and hard-hitting developmental feedback and coaching. The approach ensures two outcomes: successful strategic initiatives and a pipeline of leaders. Only this kind of action learning, which the CEO personally mentors, will provide the transformation in leadership capabilities in the compressed time frames that companies need.

That's not just a theory. In 2000, then chairperson of Hindustan Unilever, K. B. Dadiseth, launched an initiative called Project Millennium. The project included a rural distribution initiative, an Internet business, and a water-purification business. Explained Dadiseth: "These are new growth engines, which will become thriving businesses of significant size over the next six to eight years ... To develop top talent, we have put in place a process that will help identify potential business leaders much earlier in their careers than we did before. We will also create substantially more opportunities for entrepreneurial leadership ... The nine new growth engines are only the beginning. As our managers get a taste of the independent leadership opportunities that Hindustan Unilever can provide, their commitment to the company's growth will only increase." Not only did Project Millennium result in Unilever's water business and the Shakti rural distribution network, it also spawned a new generation of leaders such as incumbent Hindustan Unilever CEO Nitin Paranjpe.[5]

The idea of systematically betting on young talent by putting people in big jobs and giving them big challenges is smart. It's different from moving people on an escalator at the same pace, which is what multinational companies tend to do. Taking a bet on someone and thrusting her into a larger role is a proven process, and the only one that I know works. Despite the evidence, most leaders are conservative about taking such risks with internal talent. For some reason, it seems less risky to bet on an external hire, although the challenges, such as cultural integration and values fit, are higher.

In the future, country managers will have fewer choices; they will have to abandon conservatism and take big risks on young people if they wish to be successful. Korn / Ferry's George Hallenbeck explains why: "In India, due to the pace of growth and the size of the leadership gap, the speed at which it needs to be closed is much greater than in many other parts of the world. The result is that hyper-development is required to create tomorrow's leaders today. There are ways to do this through targeted and aggressive development efforts, but more than that, it will require leaders to take unprecedented risks with talent."

MAKE HUMAN CAPABILITY BUILDING STRATEGIC. Like all emerging markets, India has loads of bright young people with passion and potential, but there's a critical shortage of skilled talent. The skills shortage is most evident in middle management. For instance, CEOs lament the quality of their people managers, who are frequently individual contributors whom the company suddenly promotes to manage people and who lack basic skills in hiring, performance management, and coaching and development. Functional expertise, especially in disciplines like supply chain management and project management, is also in short supply. People with a general management orientation who can run a $20 million business as a profit center without hand-holding or sales leaders who can close a $200,000 deal don't exist. That isn't surprising, given how recent India's economic development is.

Building these capabilities should be easier for global corporations than it is for Indian companies, because they must exist somewhere in the global network. The challenge is to transfer expertise and capability. Some companies use joint projects as a transfer mechanism. From 1990, Cummins India deliberately moved global responsibility for engine families like the V-12 and KV series to India. Those projects became vehicles to build engineering and manufacturing capabilities in a new location. Dozens of engineers would go back and forth between the United Kingdom, the United States, and India, facilitating the transfer of expertise and learning.

Similarly, when AB Volvo wanted to develop a new value truck for emerging markets, it approached the task as a collaborative project between its headquarters in Sweden, Nissan Diesel in Japan, and Volvo-Eicher in India. The idea was to marry Eicher's frugal engineering capabilities with Sweden's technology expertise and Nissan Diesel's quality manufacturing know-how. The project has resulted in a new low-cost Asian supply base in China and India, increased engineering and manufacturing capability in India, and a better understanding in Sweden of what low cost means.

Another way of transferring knowledge is to get people, especially experts, moving around the global network. At any time at Bosch, there are nearly a hundred Indian engineers working outside the country and an equal number from other countries working in India. Some assignments might last three years, but more commonly they last less than a year. Bosch has a formal policy that encourages such movement: to become a senior executive, an employee must have worked outside his or her home country. It is also a prerequisite to have worked in multiple functions and to have led a cross-functional team. Jean-Pascal Tricoire, CEO of Schneider Electric, insists that members of the leadership team have emerging market experience. It is much the same at European consumer products companies like Unilever, L'Oréal, and Nestlé, which have consistent job levels, compensation, and other policies, so it's easy for people to move from one country to another. Some companies like Google, Goldman Sachs, Citibank, Bank of America, and DHL see volunteering as a catalyst for leadership development and send employees to work for a year or two with nonprofit organizations like Teach for India.

Companies like Bosch, Dell, Cummins, Honeywell, Ericsson, JCB, Reckitt Benckiser, and Standard Chartered base global leaders in India. That transfers knowledge and fuels aspirations. It also sends a message to ambitious young leaders that they do not have to leave India or the company to have responsibility for a big business. Moreover, it allows senior leaders to spot and mentor outstanding talent.

Building the critical capabilities to execute a more ambitious strategy in India cannot be left to the India team alone; headquarters must take the lead because capability building requires a long-term view and demands investment. If people have to wonder from whose budget the investments in talent will come, nothing will happen. Talent will be trapped geographically, negating one of a multinational's biggest advantages, namely, access to bright talent around the world. Sadly, too many companies refuse to invest even 5 percent of their wage bills in developing people and organizational capabilities, and pay many times the price in India in the form of low productivity, low commitment, and high attrition.

CREATE A WORKPLACE WITH HEART. "We are breeding mercenaries," the leader of an American technology company told me during my research, capturing perfectly what I felt, too. A century ago, Fredrick Winslow Taylor sparked a revolution with his ideas about scientific management, which entailed the breakdown of work through functional specialization into standardized, simplified, highly repeatable pieces. Embraced by Henry Ford, those ideas became the basis for modern industrial management, moved from the shop floor to knowledge factories, and automation and computerization extended them to the modern era. While providing dramatic productivity gains and better standards of living, the relentless application of these methods has resulted in workplaces that are devoid of feeling, where people are called human assets but are mere factors of production. The mindless application of quotas, forced curves, engagement scores, rule books, salary bands, scorecards and metrics, mandated diversity targets, Microsoft Outlook-generated birthday greetings, and the treatment of employees based on their classification into A, B, and C players is breeding impersonal workplaces and mercenary managers.

In such a world, fairness requires the rigid application of rules. I recollect a junior employee in India being laid off forty days before his stocks were to vest; for the only son of a dependent mother, it was a big price to pay. Could we waive the rule and allow him to leave with his one hundred shares? No, the system would not permit it. A ten-year veteran employee had to be terminated for poor performance. Does he have to empty out his desk and be escorted out by security? Yes, that's what the system stipulates. How can a salesperson, who won the chairperson's award one year and underperformed the next year by missing a target, be told to leave? (This rapid fall from grace is called "hero to zero" in the sales-driven technology industry.) If the company is going to be so transactional, mindless, and soulless, why shouldn't employees be mercenary? Why wouldn't attrition be sky-high in India?

Sadly, multinational companies are more likely to operate in a heartless fashion than are family-run Indian companies, where the patriarch plays an influential role. For all their flaws, they add a personal touch and strike at least a faint emotional connection with employees. The latter see what is dismissively termed *paternalism* as genuine concern. Indeed, there is an opportunity for companies to differentiate themselves by combining a bit of the profession-alism of a multinational with the paternalism of a family-owned business.

In the mid-1990s, for example, Tata Cummins decided to build Cummins's, and India's, first air-conditioned factory. Many in Indiana thought this to be extravagant, mocking it as the Taj Cummins, but in Jamshedpur, where summer temperatures hit 48 degrees Celsius (120 degrees Fahrenheit), a factory floor can feel like a furnace. How fair is it for factory managers to sit in air-conditioned offices while workers load heavy cylinder blocks into machines in the summer? The air-conditioned shop floor turned out to be a great investment: it was great public relations and a differentiator. It was also terrific for productivity; workers simply didn't want to leave the plant! In fact, Tata Cummins is still one of the most productive plants in the Cummins network.

In a similar vein, at Microsoft India, we fought to provide health insurance for parents and in-laws. In Seattle, it may not be obvious that in a country where parents depend on their children, employees would appreciate the benefit. It proved to be a good retention tool; parents didn't react too kindly to their sons or daughters leaving Microsoft India for another company that didn't provide them health insurance. In fact, Microsoft India's attrition rate has been consistently lower than that of its peers.

Increasing commitment is critical to retain people in India. After a round of layoffs at Cummins India around 2001, there was a lot of anger and feelings of betrayal. One of my predecessors and a founder of the company, Arun Kirloskar, offered me some advice in his usually blunt fashion: "Any fool can get rid of people. Only a real leader can do it in a way that they remain ambassadors of the company." I vowed to live up to that ideal and discovered that in any situation, except fraud or willful wrongdoing, it is possible to act in ways that actually increase employee commitment, even when letting people go.

Consider, for instance, Tata Steel, which needed to downsize its workforce in 1993, a soul-searing problem for a company that guaranteed lifetime employment. The company responded with an

uncommon solution: laid-off workers under forty years old were guaranteed their salary for the rest of their working lives. Older workers
were guaranteed amounts 20 percent to 50 percent greater than their
salary, depending on their age. If they died before retirement age,
their families would receive those payments in full until the date the
worker would have retired.

The program wasn't crazy. While the laid-off workers would get
their full salaries or more, the amounts would stay constant, instead
of rising as they otherwise would have. Besides, Tata Steel would
not have to pay payroll tax or make retirement-plan contributions.
Its labor costs began to decline after the layoffs. By 2004, Tata Steel's
workforce had shrunk from seventy-eight thousand to forty-seven
thousand, with only about a third of the reduction due to natural
attrition. Lower labor costs, combined with $1 billion in fresh invest-
ments, turned Tata Steel into a globally competitive firm.

It's not through big decisions alone that you create a caring workplace; it's through the small things. I remember once deciding to stop
the celebration of all festivals in our offices to show we were secular
and to avoid controversy. One employee immediately wrote to
remind me that "real secularism meant celebrating the festivals of all
religions, not halting celebrations." He was right; festivals thereafter
became a way of unifying people and injecting energy into the organization. Don't forget that workplaces are where people spend most
of their waking hours. They deserve to be temples, not tombs, of the
human spirit, and ensuring that doesn't take money; just courage and
heart. Leading with heart is good business.

HR: The Toughest Shoes to Fill

Leading an organizational transformation is impossible without the
expertise of a superb human resources leader. However, most HR
professionals in multinational companies are managers, immersed in

tactical issues such as compensation and benefits, overwhelmed by the challenges of staffing and retention, and mechanically implementing global processes and policies thrust on them by the global headquarters. It is rare to find an HR leader who, in addition to being functionally competent, has a good understanding of the business he supports and has developed an internal network. Not infrequently, the HR head in India is seen as a political power center, that is, as someone with the power to make or break a career, to be feared rather than trusted. That's less an indictment of the innumerable competent and hardworking HR professionals in the country and more a reflection of what companies demand of them.

Leading the HR function requires more than ensuring that there are butts in seats, hiking wages constantly, and providing Thai foot massages and gourmet food in company cafeterias. Transformational HR leaders differ from their competent counterparts in three ways: they are grounded in the business, they take a long-term approach, and they are courageous. They push leaders to focus on the people agenda, even as they push back on corporate HR to do what makes sense in India.

It may sound trite, but good HR leaders care about employees. They have to connect with people on the front line and have their fingers on the pulse of the organization. In a widely circulated article, Ram Kumar, the executive director (HR) of ICICI Bank, lamented "the decadence of our thinking, from engaging and relating to people to managing human resources. We are obsessed with high-sounding concepts, processes, tools, and metrics, but have lost sight of the human being ... This resource management piece has to be substituted by a people relationship focus."[6] Added another senior HR leader: "The HR profession does need to reflect on why it is so criticized. Does it have empathy with people or has it got caught up in processes and paperwork? Indians grow up in a caring environment at home and expect somewhat similar treatment at work. HR is expected to be a torchbearer of employee issues but has neglected that aspect by becoming mechanical."[7]

A multinational company's HR leader in India must take guidance but have the courage to do only what is right for the local organization. That means implementing compensation and benefits that make sense in India and fighting for designations and titles that matter locally. Rather than implementing the global blueprint with narrow, fragmented roles and multiple reporting lines, creating a locally relevant structure with big jobs will help attract talent and grow leaders. This is critical because multinationals increasingly compete with Indian companies for top talent. Even Hindustan Unilever, traditionally a magnet for talent, has had trouble retaining good leaders because "jobs at HUL are becoming more functional and narrow," reported the *Economic Times* quoting a senior executive.[8]

Senior executives increasingly flee multinationals for opportunities in Indian companies, braving the challenges of divergent value systems and less professional environments for a piece of the action. "Moving from a regional role in an MNC, where empowerment is low and decision making is slow, to having P&L responsibility, complete ownership, and direct access to the chairman is enormous motivation," admits a senior executive who recently made the switch.[9]

The HR leader also has to help transform a set of talented individuals into a leadership team, which is particularly challenging in India. "An emphasis on individual achievement right from childhood breeds leaders who are capable but competitive, rather than collaborative, and who define success in individualistic terms. They are highly capable lone wolves and we have to teach them to hunt in a pack," points out Hindustan Unilever's Leena Nair. HR experts like Nair make an enormous effort to become coaches to the country manager and his or her top management team, helping members individually as well as facilitating their growth as a team.

Given the shortage of smart HR leaders, Indian companies are turning to business heads to lead HR. At Wipro, Pratik Kumar is not only the senior vice president of HR but also leads Wipro's infrastructure engineering business. At the AV Birla Group, Santrup Misra is the group HR leader but also heads the carbon black business. And M&M Group's Rajeev Dubey leads both HR and the aftermarket business. Multinational companies don't take such risks, although there's one exception that proves the rule: at Bosch India, A. Krishnan spent seven years running a factory before taking on the HR role. Multinationals should encourage this kind of mobility to create more HR leaders.

Why Culture Doesn't Matter

Many executives believe that because there are profound cultural differences, managing in India takes different skills and approaches. In my experience, there's no distinctive "India Way" that yields magical results. All it takes is focus, discipline, and a long-term commitment to becoming a talent factory. Hold leaders accountable for growing leaders, take big bets on young stars, invest strategically in developing important capabilities, hire a courageous leader to be the HR partner to the business, and the sputtering talent engine will roar to life. Anything short of that and the results will be disappointing.

In "Why Globalization Will Revolutionize Talent Management," Nitin Nohria, dean of Harvard Business School, wrote:

> Research shows that innovation is driven by problems that become very pressing. Japanese manufacturing, for example, became efficient because it was driven by that nation's limited access to raw materials. The huge demand for talent in emerging markets is a similar pressing problem that demands innovative solutions. As I watch developments in India and China, I wonder whether these countries will drive the new best practices for

talent management much as Japan's lean manufacturing system became the best practice for manufacturing. The companies that succeed will not necessarily be Indian or Chinese; they could well be American or European. The winners, as Darwin noted, will not be the strongest firms today but those who are the most adaptive in the years ahead.[10]

Thus, the challenges of growing talent in India are monumental, but precisely because India is so challenging, like China, it may well be the petri dish for developing next-generation leaders. Companies should approach the task in that spirit.

THE TAKEAWAYS

- A young, emerging economy, a decade of good growth, and a weak educational system have created shortages of every kind of talent, especially functional experts and leaders. Leaders must move from relying on professional hiring and anemic development efforts to a commitment to grow talent from within.

- What works is holding leaders accountable for developing young leaders, making significant investments in building critical people capabilities, creating a workplace with heart, and promoting a leader to head the HR function.

- The best developers of leaders do two things:

  1. They take big bets on promising leaders. They give them big jobs or big missions and use those as crucibles for strengthening leadership capability.

  2. They integrate strategy development and people development. Key strategic initiatives are led by

next-generation leaders and staffed with young high-potential talent. Senior leaders are deeply involved with these initiatives and use this to evaluate and coach.

- Companies must approach building the critical capabilities to execute an ambitious strategy in India consciously and strategically. They cannot leave it to the team in India, however competent that team may be. While the process has to be collaborative, headquarters must take the lead, because building capabilities requires investments and a long-term view.

6

India as an Innovation Lab

*The old paradigm was think global, act local. At Hindustan Unilever,
we've turned it on its head. We think local—and act global.*

—NITIN PARANJPE, CEO, HINDUSTAN UNILEVER

Imagine that you're the largest purchaser and seller of beef in the
world. How would you create a national, fast-growing, and profitable
restaurant chain in the world's second-most-populous country? What
would you do if that market happens to be largely vegetarian and
poor, a country with its own rich culinary heritage, where cows are
sacred, and where $1 (Rs. 55) is a chunk of change? McDonald's is a
good example of a global company that has not just customized or
adapted its offerings and business model for India, but has taken its
global expertise in branding, supply chain, restaurant management,
and business processes and married it with local entrepreneurship,
frugality, and innovation to create an extraordinarily successful
business in India.

In 1995, McDonald's entered the country by setting up joint ventures
with two partners-turned-franchisees, Hardcastle Restaurants and
Connaught Plaza Restaurants. McDonald's India has been growing fast

and plans to expand its outlets from 275 in 2012 to 500 by 2015. "How did you pull that off?" I asked Amit Jatia, the forty-year-old entrepreneur who manages the franchise in southern and western India. He replied: "Glocalization, in a word. We couldn't cut and paste business models from other countries, but we needed to bring the McDonald's brand and its expertise in supply chains and restaurant operations to India, and combine it with local requirements and culture."

At the outset, the Indian partners had to convince McDonald's that to succeed in India, it would need an entirely different menu, low price points, and a highly localized business model. Customer feedback had shown that many Indians would not even enter a restaurant that served beef or pork. India therefore became the first country in the world where McDonald's does not offer beef or pork items. Other than fries, beverages, the McChicken sandwich, and the Filet-O-Fish, there is little in common between a McDonald's in Bangalore and one in Boston. The separation of vegetarian and nonvegetarian products is maintained throughout the stages of procurement, cooking, and serving. Each outlet in India cooks the vegetarian products separately, using dedicated equipment and utensils. Even the mayonnaise and soft-serves in India do not contain eggs, and McDonald's India uses vegetable oil as a cooking medium. In August 2012, McDonald's made news by opening its first two all-vegetarian restaurants in India.

It took McDonald's and its partners five years to figure out a customer value proposition and business model that would deliver results in India. Called "branded affordability," the strategy is to keep prices low while making profits. McDonald's introduced a Happy Price Menu for Rs. 20 (around $0.40) and refined its Indian business model to make profits on it. Since McDonald's is a high-volume, low-margin business, both Jatia and Vikram Bakshi, the franchisee for north and east India, figured out that at that price, sales would have to be three to four times US store sales to break even. Since that was not likely initially, they had to find a way to reduce costs while maintaining global food safety norms and customer service standards.

McDonald's identified the must-haves in India as safe food and one-minute service. Everything else was only nice to have, so they eliminated most of it. For instance, the Indian franchisees localized most of the equipment, except for a few key pieces. For instance, McDonald's specifies food-grade stainless steel under the counters, but the India team, realizing that was not critical for food safety, replaced it with less expensive material. The team found a lot of excess equipment, such as large vats, in the standard store design, so it developed three formats based on store size. Such tweaks together brought down the investment in each store by between 30 percent and 50 percent.

The India team also brought down taxes in several ways. For instance, branded fries attract a 20 percent excise duty, but McDonald's India saved that by removing the supplier's name. Similarly, it found that transporting chopped lettuce and milk shake mix attracted duties from the city government, but lettuce heads and milk didn't do so. That seemed illogical, so it lobbied for change. Finding utility costs high in India, the company worked with IIT Bombay, one of India's top engineering colleges, to design a system that recovers waste heat to boil water and to reduce the power consumed by air conditioners in each outlet by 25 percent. Electronic ballast for all lighting and LED signs reduced costs further. All this saved about 20 percent to 25 percent in power costs. Such systematic examination of costs allowed the Indian partners to become profitable despite the low prices they charge Indian consumers.

McDonald's success is also due to its supply chain. It spent six years and around $90 million (around Rs. 450 crore) to set up a food chain in India well before opening its first restaurant. Creating the cold chain involved the import of state-of-the-art food processing technology from its international suppliers. It has brought about major changes in vegetable farming, benefitting India's farmers.

At first, suppliers were few, and in some product categories, such as iceberg lettuce and potatoes, they were nonexistent. For instance, the kind of potato McDonald's uses was then unavailable in India. Farmers used seeds from the preceding crop, which resulted in a single variety of poor-quality table-grade potatoes. The company needed process-grade potatoes, which are long, have a high solid content, and low moisture content. Its supplier partner, McCain Foods, worked closely with farmers in Gujarat and Maharashtra to develop process-grade potato varieties. Working with agronomists, McCain introduced irrigation systems, sowing treatments, planting methods, fertilizer application programs, and better storage methods. McDonald's global partner, OSI, set up a dedicated unit in India, Vista, for making potato patties. Vista sells its products to several other food brands.

With support from other international partners, McDonald's ensured that lettuce was grown widely. A local partner, Ramakrishna Foodlands, set up a cold chain that includes refrigerated trucks and temperature-controlled distribution centers. "McDonald's was fantastic in transferring know-how," says Smita Jatia, Amit's wife and the managing director of Hardcastle Restaurants. To learn the McDonald's way, the start-up team went through a month-long training program in Indonesia. A global team then flew to India to figure out every aspect of the business. McDonald's India hired people with high school degrees and invested millions of dollars in training them in Chicago and Asia. That investment has paid off in commitment and performance.

The final element of McDonald's success came from investing heavily in creating a trusted and aspirational brand. The challenge was to change consumer perceptions from American don't-know-what-to-expect discomfort to Indian values, families, culture, and comfort. In short, it's a friendly place where families can enjoy themselves and feel they are having a special time. The team designed everything around this—from the menu to the layout and décor.

After McDonald's started advertising in 2000, global ads quickly gave way to local ones with campaigns like *Bees Mein Dhamal* (which translates literally as A Big Bang for Twenty Bucks) and McDonald's: *Har Chhoti Khushi Ka* Celebration (McDonald's: The Perfect Place to Celebrate Life's Smallest Joys). In fact, McDonald's India has spent $100 million on advertising and communications to build its brand in India over the decade.

India's Innovation Culture

As the McDonald's India example shows, India has become a wellspring of innovation. A spate of articles and books asserts that Indian companies in particular have become adept at coming up with products and services that are affordable without sacrificing quality or functionality. Offering cars for $2,500, $20 cellphones, telephone calls at a cent a minute, and open-heart surgery at $500, Indian innovators are poised to take on Western companies in much the same way Japanese companies have done over the last fifty years. Learn to excel at the game, executives are warned; ignore it at your peril.[1]

The theory is simple and compelling. Even with rising prosperity, most products and services from the developed world cater only to the top 10 percent of the developing world—the super-premium and premium segments. Those goods and services are a stretch for the aspiring middle class and are out of the reach of millions of poor people. However, the big opportunity for companies Indian and Western isn't the bottom of the pyramid, but the rapidly growing middle market, which could be nearly $1 trillion in size by 2020.[2] This segment is very demanding and driven by the desire for value for money. Middle-market customers have limited disposable incomes but big aspirations; they will not accept products that compromise quality or functionality. That's true not just of cellphones, fast foods, and shampoos but of trucks and tractors, too.

Competing for the middle market is hard. It requires developing a product or service that typically provides 70 percent of the value at 30 percent of the price.[3] Companies can't offer cheap, poor quality, or nearly obsolete products as they once did; they have to design the offering to be state-of-the-art. Companies can achieve that by value-engineering premium products or stripping away the bells and whistles, but often success requires rethinking and innovating the offer, the business model, and the distribution system.

Doing so requires a different mind-set and an intimate understanding of the customer. Therefore, companies can't develop it in New York or Paris, but in India; east for east, as Honeywell calls it. Since such products have appeal beyond India, and even in the developed world, the made-for-India products and capabilities that companies develop often serve them well globally, as reverse innovation or innovation blowback.

While several products are better marketing stories than commercial successes, a small number of successful innovations have been born in India. For instance, in 1999, Cummins India saw demand for medium-sized and large generator sets flattening, but demand for smaller diesel generator sets, between 10 and 125 kilovolt amps (kVA), was strong and growing by 25 percent, driven by residential construction, growth of telecom networks, and modern retail. As Cummins India's CEO, I felt we had to become a leader in this segment, even though the existing business model, our engines, and a service network designed for selling more expensive sets of between 500 and 2,000 kVA, would not make us competitive in that market.

In a separate division, with a dynamic twenty-five-year-old as the head, we created a new business model. Since Cummins did not have competitive small engines, the team took the heretical decision to source engines from Tata Motors and Simpson. The team designed standardized generator sets that would plug and play. It assembled the sets at high volumes in an ultra-low-cost facility in a tax-free zone, using a new distribution and low-cost service model. The generators were branded Cummins and had lower noise levels and better fuel efficiency and reliability. They revolutionized the price-performance equation in the market, and by 2008, Cummins was assembling twenty-five thousand units a year, had a 30 percent share of the segment, and was creating new capacity to export those sets globally. India became Cummins's hub for small generator sets, which has allowed the company to become one of the leading players in the segment globally.

Similarly, Deere & Company realized by 2007 that it had a problem in the Indian tractor market, the world's largest, at three hundred thousand units a year. Small tractors of less than forty horsepower made up half the market, and Deere didn't have a product in that segment. Meanwhile, market leader Mahindra & Mahindra (M&M) was leveraging its 40 percent share in India to challenge Deere in many other parts of the world. M&M's website proudly stated that "Mahindra Tractors Is the World's Largest Tractor Company by Volume," and its "Deere John" ads took Deere head-on.

Deere's leadership realized that if the company couldn't take on M&M in its home market, it would face a major problem worldwide. They launched a priority mission to develop a small tractor that could compete head-on with M&M's products. The resulting thirty-five-horsepower Deere 5000 series tractor, developed in India from a clean sheet of paper, has helped the American giant wrest nearly 10 percent of the market share and is now successfully exported to other markets.

In 2000, Hindustan Unilever initiated several entrepreneurial projects under an initiative called Project Millennium. One targeted the nearly 2 billion people who lack access to safe drinking water; unsafe water kills nearly a million Indians annually. Unilever managers saw a global opportunity in providing safe and affordable drinking water through a simple low-cost water-purification and storage device. Unilever had never been in this business anywhere, and the company had never made a consumer durable product. HUL's Pureit water purifier, which starts at Rs. 1,000 ($20), delivers safe drinking water that meets US Environmental Protection Agency standards. It is already the local market leader, growing at 30 percent CAGR, and Unilever is on its way to creating a sustainable business that will protect 500 million lives by 2020.[4]

Innovate in India for India

Despite the exceptions, there are few commercially successful innovations that multinational companies have developed in India. Vijay Govindarajan and Chris Trimble explain why, despite the hype, there are relatively few success stories.[5] The biggest hurdles aren't the market, technology, or finances; they are managerial and organizational, they argue. Most leaders haven't bought into the importance of innovating for India in India. They share several fears: product proliferation, cannibalization of high-margin products with value for money offerings, fear of diluting the brand, lowering margins—all that ensures that innovation continues to be centralized at headquarters.

Indeed, innovating for India requires a shift in the company's mental model or "the unifying logic of the company," as C. K. Prahalad wrote in "How to Be a Truly Global Company."[6] One reason that companies like McDonald's, Unilever, and Cummins have been successful is that they have moved to a new unifying logic for a common purpose and a set of core competencies in branding, procurement, distribution, and operations that yield differentiation and a cost advantage. Country organizations are free to innovate around this core.

For example, Hindustan Unilever's managers saw its competencies as understanding consumer needs, managing distribution, and creating and managing brands. They applied the competencies to a new business—drinking water. Cummins saw its core capabilities as understanding generator set applications, engineering, manufacturing, distribution, and service—not just engines. That's why it was able to buy engines from competitors and create a new business. In the old model, decision makers sat at headquarters and tried to sell more of the products they made in India. Now, decision makers sit in India, look at new opportunities, and ask how they can go after them by using global assets and capabilities.

However, even when companies bravely attempt to innovate in India, their efforts often result in a graveyard of fascinating ideas, failed pilots, crushed dreams, and truncated careers. Many promising ideas never get a fair chance of success. Dreamed up by clever people in an offshore R&D center, they don't connect with the market, succumb to bureaucracy, or get aborted by the organization. To innovate successfully for the Indian market, I find that seven factors really matter.

1. A START-UP CULTURE. Getting the innovation team set up for success, housed in the right place with the right leadership, is often a major determinant of success. The more radical the innovation, the more important it is to establish the team as a separate unit with end-to-end accountability for success. The team must have the freedom to operate like a start-up, without unnecessary bureaucracy and constraints.

Cummins India housed the small generator sets business, which I discussed earlier, in a subsidiary company, so the culture, rules, and policies of the mature business wouldn't compromise it. Power Systems India, as it was then known, had its own HR policies, could choose its vendors, and set up its own distribution network. We reintegrated it with Cummins India only after it had reached a certain size. Unilever has taken the same approach with its Pureit team, which until recently reported directly to the CEO. Managers acknowledge that progress would have been much harder had the team been part of the organization; they would have had to discuss and question every step, distracting the team from its mission.

The leaders who drive such missions are extraordinary people. I spoke to Yuri Jain, who has been part of the Pureit team from its inception in 2000 and has been leading it for several years now. Pureit is not a job for Jain; it is a mission. It isn't a ticket to a bigger mission either; Pureit is pretty much the big job for Jain. He focuses on creating a sustainable and profitable business that will protect 500 million lives by 2020. Such leaders eschew traditional badges of success for job satisfaction. "The leader has to be more self-referential, and less worried about his career, appreciation, and recognition," says Jain. Since such projects encounter a lot of difficulties and uncertainty, it is critical to have leaders like Jain who are motivated by the mission and can inspire others with it.

Not surprisingly, Jain focuses a lot on people and culture. "I hired people who were motivated by being part of something much bigger; the mission of wanting to protect lives. Many have stayed with the project for eight years, on average, working through many challenges. They need to have passion and are lateral thinkers, approaching problem solving with creativity. As the leader, I constantly question the status quo and give new ideas the space to flourish. It is vital to provide the team with air cover in difficult moments. It is important to celebrate success and learn from failure," says Jain, adding, "Give people bigger jobs and responsibility than their CVs might suggest they are ready for. Exponential growth can only happen if people grow exponentially, but that means they should have the space to grow." The best and the brightest are often drawn to such environments, suggesting that a company's ability to attract talent depends on its being able to set up innovation missions.

2. DEEP INSIGHTS, A KILLER VALUE PROPOSITION, AND A PROFITABLE BUSINESS MODEL. The single most important driver of success is getting the value proposition right, establishing the right price points, and figuring out how to make money at those price points. To succeed, companies must immerse themselves in the local market, live in the customer's shoes, and sweat the details until they find a winning strategy, even if it takes years. McDonald's took nearly ten years to crack the code of success, while Cummins' small generator sets business took five years. After a decade, Unilever's Pureit does not yet appear to be profitable although the company says it is "on track."

Consumer goods companies seem to be better at developing designs for emerging markets than are industrial and high-tech companies because they take the trouble to understand Indians. People often wonder why South Korean companies like Samsung excel in India. J. S. Shin, the president of Samsung Electronics SW Asia, shared his calendar with me, which shows the enormous amount of time he personally spends visiting consumers' homes and small retailers. South Korean product planners and engineers spend months in India visiting homes, seeing how products are used, and understanding consumer preferences. That allows them to develop TVs with menus in Hindi and other local languages, microwaves with one-touch buttons for Indian recipes, and refrigerators that withstand voltage fluctuations, have large vegetable compartments, and small freezers, which Indians prefer.

Godrej, the Indian consumer durables giant, recently introduced a refrigerator called *Chotukool* (The Little Cooler) for low-income Indian families, which has won awards, although not sales. The Godrej team leader spoke about the fishbowl principle: you can't understand the life of a fish unless you dive into the water. He also described how, in the early stages, the team spent enormous amounts of time in the field to gain deep insights into the habits and lives of poor people in rural and urban India.

The Chotukool team realized that space is precious at the bottom of the pyramid; most families live in dwellings that are only 150 square feet. Consumers purchase food a day at a time, although they do want to store some milk, vegetables, and fruits. For the tiny kiosklike shops that sell snacks, medicines, flowers, and soft drinks, an inexpensive refrigerator would be an asset, since it would enhance shelf life and reduce waste. Through immersion and observation, the team developed a 43-liter solid-state cooler that uses no compressor or refrigerants, and since there is often no electricity, it works on a battery or solar power. The fridge is light enough to move around the house; keeps food fresh and cool; and at $60, costs less than half the cheapest conventional model.

At Hindustan Unilever, consumer immersion has become a religion. It sees its future in a small phone booth called Voices from the Street. An oddity in the company's sprawling campus in Mumbai, the glass booth has a telephone, a headset, a table, and a chair. HUL's 981 executives must each spend fifteen minutes in the booth every week, listening to consumers rave, rant, request, and make suggestions.

Many consumer conversations lead to decisions. For example, HUL put usage instructions on its Dove Facial Serum packaging based on a consumer's suggestion to CEO Paranjpe. Similar insights spurred HUL to come up with permeable packaging for soaps (Indians like to sniff at soaps before buying them), and because water is scarce, detergents that reduce water consumption and rinse times by 50 percent.

Innovation teams are increasingly turning to social scientists and ethnographers to gain deeper consumer insights. In 2006, a team of researchers from Microsoft Research in Bangalore spent several days in schools that teach poor children. They found only four PCs in a classroom of forty children, so ten students crowded around each machine. Within each group, the brightest, richest, or oldest child would take charge of controlling the mouse. While other students pointed, gestured, and reached out, they had no control of the PC and inevitably lost interest. The child with the mouse learned, while the others didn't.

Conventional wisdom suggests that the solution was for schools to buy more PCs, thereby boosting the PC-to-student ratio (and increasing software sales). Many schools in developing countries can't afford more PCs, though, and traditional PCs don't allow for collaborative learning. Microsoft researchers therefore developed a creative solution. Called Windows Multipoint, the software lets several users share a single PC with multiple mouses or other devices, and to learn collaboration skills as well. The technology helps shift students from passive to active learning, and the collaborative environment adds a new layer of value to PCs in classrooms. Multipoint offers a more affordable way to decrease student-to-PC ratios and provides a platform for Windows education software developers to create collaborative learning applications. Building on its insights about shared computing, Microsoft introduced Windows Multipoint Server in 2010. The server version enables multiple users to each run different applications on their own stations, shrinking the cost of managing technology infrastructure. The product, which is gaining traction in schools worldwide, started from an insight gained in dusty classrooms in South India.

Traditional companies operate with a cost-plus mind-set that works only if you are Apple. Successful innovators have a strong design-to-cost ethos. They work backward from the price that will succeed in the segment, designing the product and the business model so they hit the sweet spot of volumes and margins. In contrast to the successes I mentioned earlier, consider one of our experiments at Microsoft India to promote the adoption of PCs by bringing down the cost of software.

In 2005, we launched Windows Starter Edition for India targeting low-income, first-time PC users. With an original equipment manufacturer (OEM) price of around $20, Starter Edition had some useful features, such as detailed help menus, but came with restrictions on the processor and a limit of three concurrent applications running, and so on. It was an interesting experiment but failed to gather any traction. Our mistake was to focus only on bringing down the price by defeaturing the product; Indian customers expect value for money, not just a cheap price. Besides, a pirated copy of Windows Enterprise edition with no restrictions was then available for less than $2.

There was a silver lining, though. In 2008, when global sales of Netbooks took off, Linux threatened to grab share from Windows worldwide. By quickly adapting Windows Starter Edition, Microsoft increased its share in the Netbooks market to over 90 percent. Had Microsoft not gained some experience with the Starter Edition in places like India, it would have been much more vulnerable to Linux.

3. ASPIRATIONAL GOALS, EXPERIMENTATION MIND-SET. Most successful innovation attempts begin with ambitious and clearly articulated missions. For instance, Ratan Tata came up with the mission to create a safe, affordable, and dignified form of transportation for Indian families of four and five members, who could only afford a scooter. That led to the Rs. 1 lakh ($2,000) Tata Nano. Dhirubhai Ambani, the founder of Reliance Industries, is widely credited with ensuring that phone calls became affordable. He articulated Reliance Communications' mission as making a phone call less expensive than buying a postage stamp. Hindustan Unilever's Pureit project started with a mission of "sustainably protecting 500 million lives by providing access to clean drinking water as safe as boiled water."

Market-driven mission statements, which describe the value to the customer rather than financial goals, align everyone around what success will look like. The ridiculously high aspirations they articulate force teams to abandon safe approaches and think out of the box. The late C. K. Prahalad was fond of saying that the primary driver of innovation is a mismatch between ambition and resources; you can either constrain resources or increase ambitions. A senior Unilever executive expanded on this idea:

Take our drive to treble our rural distribution coverage. Over the years, we had been adding a small number of outlets and patting ourselves on the back saying we were ahead of our competitors. However, they were narrowing the gap. We discovered that most people don't achieve much when you give them a slightly higher target; they operate out of a fear of failure. The trick is to think in terms of targets that put ambition so much in excess of resources that you just eliminate the fear of failure. We came up with an ambitious plan to add 500,000 more outlets in a year when we had been adding 15,000–20,000 outlets until then. In hindsight, it was an irrational decision, but look at what we achieved. Every employee knew that if we added 400,000 instead of 500,000 outlets, we would still be heroes. But if we had asked people to get to 25,000 and they managed only 20,000, we would have thought that they had failed and they would too.

Successful teams tend to follow lean start-up principles. The central tenet of lean thinking is to think big, start small, fail fast, and scale quickly. That entails creating prototypes to test market assumptions rapidly and using customer feedback to develop them faster than through traditional product development practices. It enables early, rapid, and less costly corrections of assumptions and therefore can help decrease the time and cost for a new business to gain market traction. Eric Ries, an evangelist for the lean start-up movement, articulates the difference: "A lot of new business ventures, especially within established firms, start with an assumption that the customer is known and what they want are reasonably known and the growth will happen through good execution. However, the environment in emerging markets is much more uncertain with rapid unanticipated changes. A better paradigm is to assume that customers, features, pricing are all unknown. Winning comes from learning and iterating fast through continuous cycle of interactions with the market and moving faster than competitors do."[7] That's how McDonald's India continues to drive innovation in its menu, store formats, and new conveniences like cashless checkouts. Pushing his team to innovate faster, Amit Jatia directs them to test new ideas in the real world rather than debate them in conference rooms. He also encourages them to ask for forgiveness rather than permission.

4. AN ASPIRATIONAL BRAND THAT PEOPLE TRUST. Success in scaling an innovation requires significant thought and investment in establishing an aspirational brand. Companies often obsess over the product, but fail to invest in building the category and the brand. Even the most creative innovations will fail without the necessary investments in brand. GE's low-cost electrocardiogram and ultrasound machines represent breakthroughs, but GE may have relied too much on public relations rather than marketing to deliver the message.

One company that hasn't overlooked the importance of establishing a brand is Hindustan Unilever. As I described earlier, it created the drinking-water-purifier category in India and sold the Pureit brand through large investments in a direct-sales force. However, lower-cost, low-efficacy competitors soon stole market share from it. To differentiate itself on the core attribute of safety, HUL issued a safety challenge. It would give a prize of Rs. 1 crore ($200,000) to anyone who demonstrated a water purifier that was as effective as Pureit. For three years, no one has been able to claim the prize. HUL has created a campaign around the challenge, which has cemented its leadership.

It's possible to build a brand without a huge budget. Volvo Bus has changed the face of the industry in India. According to Akash Passey, Volvo India's CEO, who personally built the bus business in India, "fourteen years ago, it was nearly impossible to sell a bus for Rs. 50 lakh [$100,000] in a market where the maximum price-tag was Rs. 10 lakh [$20,000]. When we introduced Volvo buses, people appreciated how quiet the bus was; they routinely mistook speeds of 80 kmph to be

50 kmph." Passey hired college interns to accompany each bus, which ensured continuous passenger feedback. He would know of problems even before the bus operators did. Volvo identified bus drivers as critical in maintaining the buses and providing the travel experience. It started training drivers even before selling the first bus, calling them coach captains, and anointed them its ambassadors.

Volvo Bus spread slowly across India, ensuring that service and support grew in tandem with sales. Starting in southwest India, Volvo India took four years to become a national player. According to Passey, "fleet operators owners noticed that Volvo buses could operate for long distances without the need for maintenance breaks, so two could do the job of three." In addition, the service could be branded, which commanded a premium. In India, Volvo has become shorthand for safe and luxurious public transportation. Simply writing "Volvo" on the side of any vehicle allows the driver to charge a premium.

5. A GLOBAL NETWORK. A multinational company can win in India against fast and hungry local competitors only if it can leverage its global assets in a thoughtful way. It cannot win by replicating its global products and models, nor can it do so by leaving the Indian business to do its own thing. Increasingly, multinational companies find success by enabling their leaders in India to create new businesses by leveraging the assets of the global system and then replicating them globally.

McDonald's India's local partners were quintessential Indian entrepreneurs who saw the opportunity and the need for a low-cost business model. However, they had to leverage McDonald's expertise in building a brand, developing and managing a supply chain, running restaurant operations, and so on. McDonald's transferred capabilities from Chicago and franchisees in Vietnam, the Philippines, and Dubai as well as suppliers like McCain Foods. Without their support, McDonald's India would not have grown into a 270-outlet chain. Cummins India succeeded in the small generator sets business because of engineering help from Cummins Inc., which also supplied key components like alternators and controls. The parent also provided access to other markets, which ensured economies of scale. The same is true of Hindustan Unilever's Pureit, developed with the help of corporate R&D in Europe and sold in Brazil and Indonesia. As GE's John Flannery puts it:

$$\text{Success} = \text{Indian innovation} + \text{global assets/capabilities} + \text{global distribution}$$

6. DISTRIBUTION, DISTRIBUTION, DISTRIBUTION! Distribution makes all the difference in determining whether product innovations remain a curiosity or ring up the cash register. GE's much publicized MAC ECG and VIVID ultrasound system have failed to gain traction in the market, despite being between 50 percent and 80 percent cheaper than rivals, because of distribution problems. (GE is now rapidly correcting this.) Similarly, the $2,500 Tata Nano car has had disappointing sales because of a weak dealer network.

In a market with poor infrastructure and underdeveloped retail systems, innovations in distribution may be more important than product innovation. Dell India, for example, sidestepped the traditional national, regional, and retail distribution model to follow one that insurance companies use. Thousands of registered sales affiliates reach out to would-be Indian customers and give them a firsthand product experience at home or in offices.

Had Dell followed competitors, it would have had to change its built-to-order model. The result would have been a squeeze on margins, extended credit lines, and rigid incentive structures. Instead, Dell opened thirty-eight stores across India and joined hands with retailers such as the Tata Group's Croma and Future Group's eZone to set up shop-in-shop counters. It franchised the outlets to sales affiliates, who are also responsible for supporting field affiliates.

"These affiliates became an extension of Dell's offices in a region," explains Mahesh Bhalla, executive director, Dell India.[8]

Dell India backed the hybrid model by extending on-site service, initially offered only to enterprise and government accounts, to small business and individual customers in 650 locations. The new model worked, giving Dell access to even rural markets where customers aren't able to order online. Dell is growing at over 50 percent in India—faster than in any other market—and has overtaken Hewlett-Packard as the market leader.[9]

Hindustan Unilever also thinks strategically about distribution. When it launched the Pureit water purifier, it realized that many Indian households didn't understand the importance of safe drinking water, let alone the differences between a candle filter and reverse osmosis. People drank tap water until they were sick; then they drank boiled water until they recovered. Since consumer education was going to be essential to establish the product category, HUL created a five-thousand-strong direct sales force, entailing a $5 million to $10 million investment, over the less expensive traditional retail model. Only in 2010, after establishing the category, did it switch to retail distribution. Although replacement purification kits are available in retail stores, recognizing the lack of the do-it-yourself ethos in India, HUL still offers home delivery through two thousand partners. They account for as much as 50 percent of kit sales.

Many companies like GE and Microsoft India have pushed promising innovations through traditional distribution channels and killed them. For example, in 2007, to spur PC usage, Microsoft India came up with an innovative offering called IQ. Aimed at school-age children, the IQ PC came bundled with Windows, Office, Encarta, and education content from a host of partners. The content focused on Indian families' concerns, such as learning English, tutoring for open entry examinations, and ensuring a seamless transition from class work to homework. The IQ PC linked with Microsoft's MSN portal where the MSN IQ Education Channel offered more content, online tutoring, and counseling services through partners like Tutor Vista.

While the offering was comprehensive, creative, and effective when tested, it failed to take off, mainly because of a failure in distribution. Microsoft relied on OEMs to sell the IQ PC, but they only knew how to push boxes; they didn't have the marketing muscle, selling capability, or the margins to make the IQ PC a success. A better model would have been to strike partnerships with educational institutions. Instead, after a year during which we sold just two thousand IQ PCs, we had to pull the plug on the program.

7. THE "NO EXIT" POLICY. Game-changing innovations take time and enormous tenacity before they scale, and it is no different in emerging markets like India. They require the personal commitment of the CEO if they are to survive. Mukesh Ambani, chairman and CEO of Reliance Industries, calls it the no-exit policy, a version of "burn the ships." At Reliance Industries, abandoning a major innovation project is not an option; Ambani expects teams to learn from failure and keep adapting until they succeed. His responsibility is to provide them air cover and resources until they do so.

Ratan Tata, under whose watch the Tata Group has become a prolific innovator, takes the same view. Commenting on the disappointing sales of the Nano after five years, he candidly admits that Tata Motors has made mistakes, but exudes confidence that it will succeed. "I don't consider the Nano to be a flop; I believe that we have wasted an early opportunity. The launches of similar small cars vindicate our belief that this segment was missing. We will see a resurrection," said Tata publicly in January 2012.[10]

Without a no-exit mind-set, innovation drives are doomed, as my experience at Microsoft India illustrates. By 2005, Bill Gates and some of Microsoft's senior executives realized that to succeed in India, they had to think beyond its traditional strategy. Microsoft made India the test bed for experiments in using cellphones and TV sets as computers, putting advertising on cellphones, and finding ways to make PCs more affordable through shared access.

A team led by Craig Mundie, Microsoft's chief research and strategy officer, visited India and met with India's planning commission, which sets the country's five-year economic road maps. Mundie learned how committed India was to shifting from an economy based on agriculture to one driven more by small manufacturers. India has 380 manufacturing clusters, each dedicated to a particular industry. An average cluster has roughly 4,000 companies, most of them with fewer than 20 employees. The companies in these clusters used no IT, beyond a cellphone.

Tirupur is the center of one such cluster. A town of nine hundred thousand people in Tamil Nadu, it is India's T-shirt capital. Much of the world's sweatpants and underwear is manufactured there, spun and dyed piecemeal by storefront businesses and microfactories in homes. A typical garment winds eight miles through the town, from shop to shop, before it is ready for export. Commerce is stubbornly manual and frequently chaotic, and only the biggest exporters use computers to track orders and supplies. Office managers memorize quantities of the fabric and trims they purchase, and place the orders by phone. If a manager quits, all the records go with him. DSP Knitting saw its export revenues fall from $10 million in 2001 to $2 million in 2007. DSP often lost track of customer data, such as cost estimates, proposals, and orders. "Getting an order isn't a problem. The problem is in execution," says Banupriya Senthil Kumar, managing partner of DSP.[11]

When it conducted a survey in Tirupur, Microsoft found demand for technology, but most entrepreneurs felt overwhelmed by its cost and complexity. Even though they could get a PC for $600, it would cost between $30,000 and $50,000 to set up a local network with a server loaded with business software and to find an experienced professional to manage it. That's beyond the budgets of most small

Indian businesses. From 2007 to 2008, Microsoft led a project in Tirupur to roll out an order-tracking application that knitters could access over the Web through text messaging. A partner, Affordable Business Solutions, managed all the back-end hardware and maintenance. Fees ranged from $100 to $250 per user per month. Microsoft created a technology demonstration center with twenty computers, two servers, and videoconferencing equipment, which gave live demonstrations on how a textile company could streamline its business. Eight customers signed up the day it opened, and another fifty sent letters saying they were interested.[12]

By 2012, though, this innovative project, called Vikas (or progress), had been wound down, and the team had been absorbed into the mainstream of selling Office and Windows licenses. The leader in selling affordable solutions through a pay-per-use model is Tata Consulting Services (TCS), which has set up a new division called iON. TCS competes with Microsoft's cloud-based offerings, claiming 150 channel partners, 200 customers, and a goal of earning a billion dollars in five years. Despite a three-year head start, leadership for the future in Tirupur seems to have moved from Microsoft to TCS.

How did this happen? Microsoft is a rare company that is willing to take a long-term view when it comes to product innovation. It had sustained billions of dollars of losses for a decade or more until the Xbox or the Bing search engine succeeded. Trouble is, in Microsoft's model, all innovation has to happen in Redmond, Washington; countries like India are not mandated, funded, or equipped to drive business model innovation. Vikas was a skunk-works project funded out of the local India budget. A successful proof of concept was demonstrated, but when the global economy went into recession in 2008, Microsoft India was not able to support Project Vikas's scale-up or the project.

We can learn two lessons from Microsoft's experiences. One is the need for top management commitment, a no-exit policy that will allow innovation projects time to mature and scale. The other is that multinational companies need to treat geographic markets as a source of innovation. Not all innovations need to come from the centrally planned, disciplined, and expensive process that global companies follow. There should be room for bottom-up experimentation in emerging markets like India. Many creative business models develop in places like India and Kenya, so key geographies should have some freedom to innovate and modest innovation budgets to play with. That's how Cummins's small generator sets business started. That's how Pureit was born.

THE TAKEAWAYS

- In a market like India, the real opportunity for companies is not the affluent top of the pyramid or the fortune at the bottom of the pyramid; it is in the large and fast-growing middle market. That's true for consumer products as well as industrial products.

- Competing for the middle market is hard. Across categories, to win requires an offering that typically provides 70 percent of the value at 30 percent of the price. Unlike in the past, such a product cannot be cheap or of poor quality. It has to be an offering tailored so that everything that adds cost but isn't valued by the customer is stripped away. This requires product innovation. Sometimes, it may require a different business model.

- Companies must apply similar innovation to every element of the marketing mix: brand positioning and awareness, distribution, pricing, and business model. When driven by R&D, companies often overlook the importance of getting those parameters right.

- Companies find a ready market for their middle market offerings in other emerging markets and increasingly, due to deteriorating economies, in more affluent markets as well.

- While conceptually simple, the idea of innovating for the local market in India and using it as a lab for other emerging markets is challenging. It is not as simple as just asking the offshore technology center in India to develop products for the local market. It calls for the patience of a saint and the pockets of a prince, as the aphorism goes. The biggest obstacles are internal mind-sets, both organizational and managerial.

- Success requires a clear mandate, executive sponsorship, commitment, courage, an experimentation mind-set, tolerance of failure, and the ability to leverage the knowledge, assets, and capabilities of the whole corporation. Above all, it requires tenacity.

7

How to Think About Joint Ventures in India

One key reason why Cummins has succeeded in India and China is because we learned how to make joint ventures work.

—TOM LINEBARGER, CHAIRMAN AND CEO, CUMMINS INC.

Mention the term *joint venture* and most executives in multinational companies as well as Indian corporations will shudder delicately and change the subject. That isn't surprising; over the past twenty years, most joint ventures (JVs, for short) have failed, especially in emerging markets where experts estimate the failure rate at 60 percent. While several partnerships in India have ended acrimoniously—Telenor-Unitech, Britannia-Danone, and DB Realty–Etisalat, for example—in other instances, objectives diverged, the two sides were unable to work through their problems, and one eventually bought out the other. That's what happened at TVS-Suzuki, Godrej-P&G, Modi-Xerox, Tata-IBM, Mahindra-Renault, and L&T–John Deere, among others.

However, some JVs in India have been spectacularly successful. The ties between family-owned companies and MNCs such as the Kirloskars and Cummins (Kirloskar Cummins), the Munjals and Honda (Hero Honda), and the Nandas and JCB (Escorts JCB) created enormous value for both sides over a long period, and those such as Tata-Cummins, Volvo-Eicher, and Wipro–GE Healthcare endure to this day. My research and experience suggests that joint ventures either create significant value or destroy large amounts of value, and the outcome usually depends on whether companies have nurtured alliance management capabilities.

Some executives extrapolate from one bad experience, and using every horror story as further confirmation, they become permanently averse to JVs. That, I believe, is a mistake. Joint ventures, strategic partnerships, and acquisitions are all essential to succeed in emerging markets like India and China. CEOs should rely less on instinct and knee-jerk reactions, and examine these options with an open mind.

When they work, JVs offer three major benefits. One, joint ventures help multinational companies overcome the regulatory hurdles related to foreign ownership in emerging markets so they can enter markets early. For instance, retailers like Walmart and Tesco as well as insurance giants like Allianz and New York Life have used joint ventures to enter India because the government doesn't permit 100 percent ownership by foreign companies in those sectors. Similarly, in highly regulated industries such as telecommunications, mining, and defense production, foreign companies need Indian partners to help obtain licenses and permits. That's why telecom giants Telenor and Etisalat entered into alliances with real estate groups Unitech and DB Realty, for instance.

Two, a JV can help turn into reality the belief of two companies that they can reshape an industry because of their complementary capabilities. For instance, after failing to make a dent in the Indian commercial vehicles market on its own, Sweden's AB Volvo and India's Eicher Motors joined in 2008 to take on the two market leaders, Tata Motors and Ashok Leyland. Volvo brought modern technology, a global brand, and economies of scale to the table, while Eicher contributed a strong local brand, market knowledge, distribution, frugal engineering, and manufacturing capability. By 2012, Volvo-Eicher had doubled sales and operating margins in India, while growing its market share from 8 percent to 12 percent.

However, the single most important and powerful reason why a JV is often worth considering in emerging markets is simply governance. Having run a very large and successful JV for nearly a decade (Tata Cummins) and a number of smaller but equally successful ones, I am convinced that if you can find the right JV partner, $1 + 1 = 11$. It's quite simple. If you have two partners who trust each other, bring complementary assets or capabilities, and are focused on expanding the pie as opposed to worried about dividing it, the governance structure of a JV provides the freedom and accountability to its management team to take what is best in both parents and create a vibrant and valuable new business.

It isn't easy, but we were able to do that at Tata Cummins, a fifty-fifty JV set up in 1995 to provide truck manufacturer Tata Motors with Cummins's modern engine technology. Cummins provided the product platform as well as engineering and manufacturing capabilities, while Tata Motors brought an extraordinary distribution system, frugal engineering skills, and regulatory influence. The management team was young, entrepreneurial, and passionate about reshaping the truck business in India. A five-year plan laid out the products, localization level, branding strategies, pricing, and distribution strategies that would most likely succeed in India. Tata Cummins's board, which had five representatives from each side, reviewed the business every quarter on just four metrics: product cost, product quality, cash flow, and profitability. My team had complete operational autonomy. We decided marketing strategy, picked what products to offer, dropped features that added to costs but not customer value, and could add head count even if there was a hiring freeze in Indiana or Mumbai. The combination of a long-term plan, tremendous operating freedom, and accountability to the board turned out to be critical to the venture's success. Eight long years later, and after surviving a make-or-break moment, Tata Cummins delivered results.

Both Cummins of the United States and Tata Motors were seasoned and opinionated partners, but they had an equal say in managing the JV, which created a constructive tension. Neither partner was able to impose its views, so we could figure out what made sense for our venture. This governance model allowed the JV to take what was the best from each parent, yet not be bogged down by their internal bureaucracies. Thus, the structure prevented Cummins from being mindlessly global and Tata from being helplessly local. Olof Persson, CEO of AB Volvo, who oversees successful JVs with Lingong in China and Eicher in India, agrees: "JVs provide a good braking force against our instinct to want to do everything the Swedish way."

Why JVs Fail

The most common reason joint ventures fail is poor due diligence. Companies would do well to ask themselves: Does the partner share our values? Do we respect their leaders? Do our ambitions and goals align, or will they come into conflict soon? Can we trust them to do the right thing whenever we run into a roadblock? Will they stick to the letter of the deal or understand its spirit?

Some JVs fail because foreign companies are unwilling to do things differently for the India market—change pricing or customize products, for instance. That's why the Renault-Mahindra JV stumbled; Renault's CEO Carlos Ghosn admits: "The Logan [a low-cost car that had been successful in Europe and Russia] was too expensive; it was not sufficiently localized."[1] Then, in 2007, some of Mahindra-Renault's rivals lobbied successfully to get the excise duty on cars longer than 4 meters increased from 8 percent to 20 percent. Since the Logan was 4.25 meters long, Mahindra & Mahindra wanted Renault to shorten it. Renault refused to tinker with a global platform, which M&M perceived as typical Gallic rigidity. The two companies failed to resolve their differences, as I stated earlier, and in 2010, Renault licensed the Logan to Mahindra, and the partners ended their joint venture. (Incidentally, Mahindra relaunched the Logan as the Verito in 2012. Sales are reportedly strong.)

Most multinational companies have developed business models that have worked in the developed world. If they aren't willing to work with local partners to adapt those models to the India market, stresses will develop in the JV. Every JV will encounter a defining moment, and at that crucial moment, flexibility and a willingness to understand the partner's views and seek a win-win solution rather than simply throw in the towel become critical. That's how the Tata-Cummins joint venture survived (see "A Defining Moment at Tata Cummins"). Adds Cummins's Tom Linebarger: "A big reason why some JVs work while others don't is the willingness of the partners to compromise. Big egos make for lousy JVs."

A Defining Moment at Tata Cummins

In the summer of 2000, Ratan Tata, the chairman of the Tata Group and Tata Motors, was huddled in conference in a small London hotel with Tim Solso, the chairman and CEO of Cummins Inc., the US-headquartered engines giant. The two were discussing the future of their five-year-old joint venture, Tata Cummins. The atmosphere was tense.

The optimism with which the companies had started their fifty-fifty venture in 1995 had evaporated. For Tata Motors, the JV was meant to be a way of acquiring modern low-emissions engines to modernize its commercial vehicles so it could compete with the likes of Volvo and Mercedes-Benz. It could outsource its engine operations, but retain control because of its ownership stake. For Cummins, the JV was supposed to help achieve economies of scale in a strategically important segment in a major market.

The partners brought distinct and complementary capabilities. Tata Motors had a 65 percent market share of commercial vehicles, a great sales network, a powerful brand, and policy and regulatory influence. Cummins brought world-class technology, a strong brand, and an understanding of the global vehicle business. The companies had similar values, and the two chairpersons enjoyed good personal chemistry.

However, the JV, set up with a capacity of seventy thousand engines, ran into trouble almost from day one. Every assumption turned out to be optimistic: the price customers would pay, the rate at which emissions regulations would evolve, the quality and performance of the Tata vehicles with the Cummins engines, and the capability of the service network. As a result, losses mounted and the plant remained underutilized. For five years, the JV worked hard to redesign the product for India, localize manufacturing, and create distribution and service capability, but it was clear that the economics were still broken.

At the current transfer price, Tata Motors believed that the demand for the new engines would only be ten thousand units a year. To convert all Tata vehicles to the Cummins engine and fully utilize capacity would require the price to be at least 25 percent lower. Tata also believed that the JV agreement was fundamentally unfair to it. The Cummins management felt strongly that the reason for the crisis was the lack of commitment to phase out Tata Motors' engines and the partner's inability to sell the considerable benefits of the Cummins engine-equipped trucks. It also felt that it was disingenuous of Tata Motors to renegotiate the agreement; a deal, after all, is a deal.

Solso had three options. One, buy out Tata's stake in the JV, sell as many engines to Tata as it wanted, but find other customers as well. Two, stay in the JV, but rely less on Tata to use the capacity of the plant and find other customers. Three, reduce prices by 25 percent in return for a renewed commitment by Tata to change over its vehicles to Cummins engines and hope that the JV could reduce costs so it could still make money.

Overruling the advice of his senior leaders (including, I must say, me) who mostly favored the second option, Solso took a long-term view, chose the third option, and we cut the price by 25 percent. Solso agreed with Tata's view that the agreement was one-sided and would not endure. He felt that even if Cummins took a hit in the short term, it would be immeasurably better off with a strong partnership in a fast-growing market.

As a result, the JV had to embark on a massive cost-reduction plan to break at the lower price. Every feature that added cost but not value was dropped, including an electrically operated engine fan and an electric shutoff switch. The JV asked suppliers for ideas and price reductions. Within a year, the manufacturing cost fell by 35 percent and, eventually, by 50 percent, and volumes shot up.

Tata Cummins is one of the few JVs that currently survive in the Tata Group. While capacity has expanded to 240,000 engines a year, revenues are approaching $1 billion, with the return on capital exceeding 30 percent. The JV has given Cummins a 40 percent plus share of the world's second-largest truck engines market and makes a healthy contribution to global profits. It took Tata Cummins eight years to make money for its parents, and many companies would have thrown in the towel in the difficult summer of 2000. But Solso and Tata took a long-term view, working through a tough issue to their mutual benefit.

The downsides of a partnership gone sour can be traumatic and set a company's strategy back by years. For instance, Norway's Telenor entered into a partnership (Uninor) with India's Unitech only to gain access to the telecom licenses that the government of India had awarded the company in 2009. However, the sale of the licenses turned out to be part of a moneymaking racket that politicians and bureaucrats had hatched. After the India media exposed the scandal, the Supreme Court of India canceled 122 licenses, including those of Uninor and sent Sanjay Chandra, Unitech Wireless's CEO, to jail. Telenor then accused Unitech of breach of warranties, sought damages in court, and has written off a large part of its investment in the country. It's reboot time for Telenor in India.

How JVs Succeed

Clarity makes JVs succeed. A well-defined scope, a realistic business and investment plan, clear roles for each partner, and alignment on governance, performance management, and dispute resolution mechanisms in case of disagreements must all be discussed, negotiated, and clearly captured in an agreement. When Walmart teamed up with the Bharti Group to enter India, they agreed that the venture would focus only on the cash-and-carry business at first. The business plan laid out a gradual scaling up of operations, starting out in India's smaller cities, and Walmart agreed that the JV would use India-centric systems because of the operational challenges the country poses.

Similarly, the success of Volvo's commercial vehicle venture with Eicher in India is partly due to strategic clarity. The JV agreement clearly specified the management responsibilities of each partner. Volvo and Eicher also agreed on a dual branding strategy, whereby they would use Eicher for the midmarket segment and Volvo for the premium vehicles market. The business plan laid out the growth and market share objectives, the product plan, and the investments. Volvo consciously avoided integrating the JV into its fold or imposing its operating systems, while it staffed strategic projects with people from both sides. The JV is a board-managed entity, with Eicher managers in place. Since its formation, the JV has grown market share and profitability every quarter.

Managing joint ventures is a skill or a capability, and companies must work hard to develop it. Take Cummins, which has used joint ventures to do well in India and China. Cummins wasn't born with the ability to manage joint ventures successfully; partnering is a capability that the company developed because it was central to its strategy. It entered India in 1962 through a JV with the Kirloskar Group, which lasted until 1995. Then followed the Tata Cummins JV; later, Cummins struck six more JVs and three strategic partnerships with manufacturers of diesel-fueled power-generating sets. These partnerships laid the foundations for Cummins's success in India. Similarly, in China, Cummins's joint venture with Dong Feng Motors has been a game changer. Cummins has fifty-five JVs worldwide; fifty-three of them are doing well, according to Solso, the former chairperson and CEO under whose leadership many of them were formed.

The Importance of Chemistry

A JV's future hinges on the chemistry between senior executives on the two sides. One business leader compares joint ventures to India's arranged marriages, which are "full of hope but not necessarily of knowledge." Not only should the CEOs of the two companies get to know each other, but also approximately two dozen senior executives on both sides must become familiar with one another. They must make the time to have informal meals and get to know their Indian counterparts. What sports do they follow? What are their hobbies? What about their families? Western executives are often transactional; they focus on the issues and numbers, but fail to develop relationships. Such partnerships are brittle, with the two sides unlikely to have the ability to work through even simple disagreements.

CEOs, like Persson of Volvo and Cummins's Solso, underline the importance of relationships at the top to create trust and work through problems. "At the working level, things often get messy; people are imperfect, so disagreements and angst can quickly lead to suspicions and distrust. That's when the two CEOs must trust each other and cut through the confusion," points out Solso, who insists that CEOs must not leave relationship building to chance. "Create a formal structural relationship," he advocates, meaning that the two CEOs must meet twice a year as must the global and local heads of key functions such as product development, manufacturing, marketing, and sales.

Trust is the glue that holds joint ventures together; it is hard won and easily lost. The fundamental principle is that both parents must advance the JV's interests rather than their own interests. When one or both partners try to maximize only their interests, the JV is doomed. Managers will invariably try to optimize their company's interests; they believe that's what they're paid to do. They will do this by fiddling with the transfer pricing of components or restricting exports because they may cannibalize the parent's nonexistent revenues overseas. At one automotive JV in India, the foreign partner tried to discontinue a successful model and replace it with another, simply to increase its license fees. Neither parent should subsidize the JV, but any attempt to gain at the expense of the JV will erode trust. CEOs must be vigilant and stop such behavior. Says Siddharth Lal, managing director, Eicher Motors: "Enter into a JV if and only if you're happy about sharing the spoils. If all you can think of is 100 percent, the JV will be frustrating and eventually fail."

The manner in which partners deal with unanticipated developments is important for maintaining trust. Usually, JVs model key scenarios and assumptions and develop five-year business plans. However, as in the case of the Mahindra–Renault JV, despite the best forecasts and planning, something—competition, pricing assumptions, regulations—will turn out to be different. Rather than insisting that the agreement doesn't cover that contingency, the two companies must talk through the problem. That's often hard for multinational companies. They prefer to have majority stakes that they can use to ram through their views.

Does it matter whether each partner holds a 50 percent stake or if one holds 51 percent and the other 49 percent? A fifty-fifty joint venture may actually be more stable because neither partner is in a position to issue ultimatums or run roughshod over the other. Even when ownership stakes are unequal—say, 74 percent and 26 percent—it's important that the JV be managed as though the partners have equal stakes. "The actual equity structure matters only in a worst-case scenario," agrees Walmart's Scott Price. "Both sides must possess the conviction that a JV is the best way to approach the market. They must have the tenacity to work through differences rather than outvoting the other at board meetings." An alternative, in some circumstances, is a transitional joint venture, where the multinational company buys 50 percent to 74 percent of the company's equity, allows the incumbent team to run it, and, if it works out, eventually acquires all the equity.

Another factor that can erode trust is exit. Smart companies focus on a JV's success strategy rather than the exit strategy. That's critical because once executives have agreed on business plans, legal teams take over. Trained to focus on downside risks, they shift the conversation to exit strategies, worst-case scenarios, and wrangles over minor wording. The environment can quickly get corrosive. While it's important not to be naive, focusing too much on the downside is unhelpful. What matters are the partners' values and track records, which provide confidence that each will do the right thing if circumstances change.

That said, executives must recognize that most JVs are transient structures and have a finite life. For instance, the partner may only bring something of short-term value, such as helping to overcome regulatory hurdles, and cannot add anything operationally or financially. In such cases, it is best to unwind the joint venture amicably rather than allowing the situation to fester and turn acrimonious. During negotiations, the two CEOs should have a frank discussion about such possibilities and talk about an exit mechanism, the circumstances that would trigger it, and the principles that will apply so that the separation is amicable.

People Make JVs Tick

People often determine a JV's success, especially its board and management team. Companies often wrangle over the number of board seats that each partner should have. This could be important, but if something results in voting, it's a sign that trust has broken down. Far more important is the quality of the board members nominated. It's vital to have directors who may be senior but are not narrow or parochial. A board whose members have global, long-term perspectives is better able to navigate difficult issues without being stuck in entrenched positions. In my experience, it helps to appoint one or two independent elder statesmen respected by both partners. They can intervene thoughtfully when needed to ensure that the board doesn't stay polarized.

The choice of a CEO for the JV is particularly crucial. She or he must have good judgment, courage to do the right thing, good relationship skills, and the tenacity to work through issues patiently. The CEO must also be capable of utter impartiality rather than being biased toward either parent. The CEO's role is to stay relentlessly focused on what's right for the joint venture, not what's good for either parent.

There's often a lot of negotiation about which parent gets to staff which role. The chairperson is often from the local partner, and the global company nominates the CEO, for instance. There can be a lot of angst around certain positions like the CFO or purchasing head, but smart companies like Volvo and Cummins don't fuss about it. "The most important thing is that each partner puts in its best players, never people they want to get rid of. That's more important than arguing who nominates which position. It doesn't matter who the CFO is; we rotate the role to signal trust," explains Cummins's Solso.

One reason companies enter into joint ventures is learning. Sending very bright people to staff them is the key to ensuring that actually happens. Learning more or faster than partners ensures that companies retain power and influence in the JV, as Komatsu has demonstrated.[2] International joint ventures are great schools, so nominating promising leaders to their boards is a good development experience for promising global leaders.

Are Acquisitions Better Than JVs in India?

When late to a market, a company has no way of gaining critical mass except through acquisitions. With Indian companies' valuations becoming more realistic, and with the rupee weakening against the US dollar, this is not a bad moment for multinational corporations to pursue mergers and acquisitions (M&As) in India. The number of acquisitions across industries has been growing: witness Vodafone-Hutch, Daiichi-Ranbaxy, Abbott-Piramal, Disney-UTV, and International Paper–Andhra Pradesh Paper.

While acquisitions are important, they destroy more value than create value; this is true globally and in India. Acquirers face three risks. The first is the risk of paying too much. Until recently, valuations in India have been unrealistically high, and multinationals can be tempted to pay premiums. After all, that may not be much in dollar terms. However, buyer's remorse is common, as happened in the case of Vodafone's acquisition of Hutch and Daiichi's acquisition of Ranbaxy, followed by big write-downs of goodwill.

A second risk is poor governance. Many Indian companies are so opaque that normal due diligence may not uncover financial problems. Finally, the biggest risk is that the multinational will assimilate the local company, imposing its processes, policies, operating philosophies, and frequently its management, and killing or marginalizing the acquired company's brands. This destroys the competitive advantages of the local company's entrepreneurship, agility, market knowledge, or distributor relationships and therefore undermines the rational for the acquisition in the first place. Coca-Cola's acquisition of local brand Thums Up is a classic example; the American giant virtually killed the market leader, but was eventually forced to reverse course when demand for the Made in India cola simply refused to die.

By contrast, when DHL Asia acquired local courier Blue Dart, it quickly figured out that Clyde Cooper and Malcolm Monteiro, who had built Blue Dart into an Indian powerhouse, knew the rules of success better than it did. DHL placed its Indian operations under Blue Dart and let Monteiro run both companies. "The more change and integration that is required after an acquisition in India, the greater the risk. The best acquisitions are those that provide market access, done at a reasonable valuation, and where you have to do absolutely nothing in the first year. The ones where there is upheaval on day one are the riskiest," explains Walmart's Price, who then headed DHL Asia.

One company that seems to be doing M&As the right way in India is Schneider Electric, a serial acquirer that has taken over six companies, including Meher Capacitors, Digilink, APW President, Conzerv, Zicom, and a 74 percent stake in Luminous Power. M&As have dramatically increased Schneider Electric's reach to twenty-five thousand retail outlets and its portfolio of brands, and its revenues have trebled in three years to $1 billion. "Acquisitions have enabled us to get in five years to where it would have taken ten to fifteen years organically," says Olivier Blum, Schneider Electric's country president.

According to Blum, four things are important while conducting M&As in India. One, be clear about the strategy. M&A opportunities should not influence the strategy, but the strategy should drive M&A as a way of achieving the organization's goals. Two, the strategic intent should determine how tight or loose the integration of the acquired company should be. Blum comments, "We follow two different models depending on the strategic intent of the transaction. It can be a fully integrated model that starts from day one, where integration takes between three and six months until it is fully integrated in terms of HR processes, manufacturing, functioning, etc. In the second model, a transaction does not involve any integration at all. Conzerv was a fully integrated acquisition as that is how the benefits could be maximized. In the case of Luminous, we want to protect the DNA of the company—its brand, low-cost business model, and agility—because that's critical in the consumer market."[3]

Third, according to Blum, M&As always require support from the top. If senior management does not support the M&A strategy, the deal will fail. "Once you decide to go ahead with a transaction, you need to be able to act quickly and execute flawlessly. If senior management does not support the M&A strategy and does not fully empower the local team, there are many risks that will likely cause the deal to fail," says Blum. Fourth, cultural fit is critical. "So much so that even before we finalize a deal, we evaluate how likely and synergistic people integration is. If we have doubts about being able to integrate the cultures of the two organizations, the deal will not happen," adds Blum.

After closing the deal, it is critical to focus on integrating people. Blum's advice:

The first one hundred days are the most important. Our focus at this stage is totally on people: their roles, their development needs, their ambitions, etc. The biggest risk is losing people after the deal. This is especially true due to the demand-supply mismatch of talent. We have been able to retain 95 percent of the talent after our acquisitions. The credit goes to our agile process of integration, which ensures that people know their place in the new organization and feel engaged, valued, and motivated. We ensure that any employee of the acquired entity has the same benefits as that of a Schneider employee, with the same tenure from the joining date of the acquired organization. This helps establish a sense of belonging and unity.

While Schneider has been thoughtful in its approach to acquisitions, that's uncommon in India.

THE TAKEAWAYS

- Companies must entertain the idea of multiple acquisitions, strategic partnerships, and joint ventures to gain scale quickly in important new markets like India.

- Acquisitions that bring distribution processes, middle-market brands, and key capabilities can be useful. The common mistakes are overpaying, lack of due diligence, inappropriate integration, and incompatible cultures or values.

- While the track record of joint ventures in India is mixed, some have been spectacularly successful. When they work, JVs provide market access, key capabilities, and most of all, an execution model that is flexible, market-focused, and accountable.

- Forming and managing joint ventures are capabilities that multinational companies must consciously develop.

8

Developing Resilience to Deal with Corruption and Cope with Volatility

India has a lot of vitality, but an equal dose of volatility.
It's not for the fainthearted.

—D. SHIVAKUMAR, SENIOR VICE PRESIDENT
(INDIA, MIDDLE EAST, AND AFRICA), NOKIA

Corruption, uncertainty, and volatility characterize most emerging markets, especially India. Foreign companies must learn to deal with those factors by developing what I like to call *resilience*. That includes earning the trust of society, winning friends and influence, managing reputation, and dealing with corruption without being corrupt. Let's start with last first.

Managing in a Corrupt Environment

Corruption is a feature of most emerging markets, where institutions are young and fragile. As a result, these countries are unable to deal with the greed unleashed by sudden economic growth, resulting in rampant corruption and oligarchic capitalism. Historians point to America's Gilded Age between 1877 and 1893, when economic growth hid serious social problems, and hold out the hope that runaway corruption is but a temporary phase. However, in the short term, multinational companies have to develop the capabilities to do business in developing countries without violating home country laws or company policies and codes of conduct.

India has recently been grabbing headlines because of corruption, but it is far from being the most terrible country in the world in which to do business. Ranked 95 by Transparency International's Corruption Index, it may be more corrupt than Brazil (73) and China (75) are, but India is less so than other emerging markets like Indonesia and Mexico (both tied at 100). In fact, according to Transparency International, India is in the middle of the pack of emerging markets.

That said, corruption in India is high, all-pervasive, and may be increasing. According to Ernst & Young India's 2012 Fraud Survey, three-quarters of respondents in India believe that fraud has increased over the past year, and 60 percent said that their companies had fallen victim to it. For companies and managers, the threat isn't a big scam, such as the 2G Telecom Scam in 2010—(which *Time* rated the second-worst abuse of power ever, behind Watergate)—or Coalgate in 2012 (a scandal where the government allegedly handed several coal blocks to private miners without an auction, causing a large loss of revenue). What's more problematic is retail corruption, the almost inescapable web of corruption in the country, with a price list for almost every service the government provides. In 2012, for instance, the tariff ran something like this: Rs. 500 to Rs. 2,000 for a marriage certificate; Rs. 1,000 to pass a driving test; Rs. 1,500 to Rs. 2,500 to get an electricity connection; Rs. 5,000 for a truck to pass a tax checkpoint; Rs. 5,000 to Rs. 10,000 to speed up government services, and so on. Incidentally, pricing is changing from a fixed amount to a percentage of the transaction.

According to the Indian anticorruption website, www.ipaidabribe. com, 45 percent of Indians have paid bribes to the judiciary, 64 percent to the police, 61 percent to obtain registry services and permits, and 62 percent have paid off officials in connection with buying, selling, and renting land. Respondents to a recent World Economic Forum survey rated corruption as the second most problematic factor for doing business in India, with 78 percent frankly stating that their companies are highly vulnerable to corruption. According to another survey by KPMG of nearly three hundred CXOs of Indian and multinational companies (KPMG's India Fraud Survey 2012), 71 percent of companies felt that fraud is "an inevitable cost of business" and 55 percent had experienced fraud (up from 45 percent in 2010).[1]

India's environment of pervasive bribery and corruption is difficult for multinational companies because of the consequences of violating laws at home, such as the US Foreign Corrupt Practices Act (FCPA) or the UK Bribery Act.[2] Companies are increasingly liable not just for the conduct of their employees but also for bribes paid by intermediaries like consultants, agents, and JV partners. Operating in corrupt markets is therefore a rapidly rising risk. Is it possible to operate in a country like India without being corrupt? How can companies safeguard themselves? The answer lies in understanding the different types of corruption and fraud and inoculating themselves against each. Warning—some of what I have to say could be unpalatable and controversial for readers who may prefer to close their eyes rather than embrace a tough reality.

A Taxonomy of Corruption and What to Do About It

There are many kinds of fraudulent and corrupt practices, such as intellectual property (IP) infringement and data theft, regulatory noncompliance, procurement fraud, and asset misappropriation and theft, but a few of these are critical risks for a company operating in India.

BRIBES. Multinational companies are governed by the Prevention of Corruption Act of India, as well as home laws like the FCPA in the United States or the UK Bribery Act. Those laws prohibit managers from offering anything of value to a government official, political party, or party official with the intent to influence that person, or to secure an improper advantage in obtaining or retaining business. However, numerous global companies—De-Nocil Corporation, an Indian affiliate of Dow Chemical; AT Kearney India; Westinghouse Air Brake Technologies; Xerox Modicorp, the Indian affiliate of Xerox; Baker-Hughes; Pride International; and Diageo—have been caught paying bribes in India. In most cases, managers made improper payments to seek an advantage, such as getting a business contract, winning regulatory approval of a product, reduction of taxes, or the avoidance of customs duties.

Companies seldom make payments directly; the payments usually involve practices such as:

- Using agents or dealers to make payments

- Tapping unaccounted pools of cash, or slush funds created by payments to fictitious vendors, subcontractors, false expense reports, or price inflations to intermediaries that flow back to the company

- Sponsorship of foreign travel, extravagant gifts, and entertainment

- Charitable contributions to nongovernmental organizations recommended by government officials and politicians

Despite widespread corruption in India, I strongly believe that, barring a few sectors such as mining, telecom, infrastructure, or real estate, which are highly regulated or where the government controls access to resources, it is absolutely possible for companies to function without paying bribes. In the consumer (B2C) and industrial (B2B) businesses that most MNCs are in, bribery is far from a necessity; when it occurs, it often simply reflects bad judgment.

Paradoxically, it may actually be easier for a foreign company to be ethical than it is for an Indian business. A lot of multinational companies have channel-driven business models that legitimately route sales through distributors, dealers, and other value-added resellers. Many companies believe that this model offers a natural firewall against corruption. The low levels of empowerment in multinationals also offer a plausible excuse for local leaders to say that they can't do anything illegal for fear of losing their jobs. By and large, people realize that top management teams in India are mere agents with limited authority. Executives can therefore persuade them to turn their attention to easier targets. Moreover, a company that is uncompromising in its ethics over time develops a reputation that serves as a shield against corruption.

SPEED MONEY OR GREASE PAYMENTS. The distinction between bribes and speed money is simple: a bribe is a payment to a government officer for doing something he should not do; speed money is a payment for doing something he should.

Every company encounters endless demands for speed money, especially from government officials. They often create circumstances where, for routine issues such as clearing shipments, getting permits or licenses, or registering land deals, companies must make a facilitation payment or suffer inordinate delays. "From the time a businessman thinks of starting a venture, every step is paved with red tape and demands for bribes. The system makes it impossible for people to function legally. There is no time limit to issue a license or renew a permit. If I do not pay my way through, the authorities can make me wait indefinitely before processing my application. The license-permit raj may be over but the *chaipani* culture [literally, demanding money to cover the cost of buying a cup of tea] continues," says a well-known Indian businessperson.

Paying speed money is illegal in India and not permitted by the law in many countries like the United Kingdom; companies must resist the temptation to be expedient and give in to demands. However, the uncomfortable reality is that there are times when it may be difficult to avoid—think for instance of perishable goods awaiting customs clearance. This is where firms may be compelled to use intermediaries such as clearing agents who handle the whole process. The use of such agencies and intermediaries is a troubling decision and the key in these circumstances is to ensure that the transaction involved is a routine, nondiscretionary action and the company isn't seeking an improper benefit. The agency or intermediary the company uses should be reputable and provide a real value-added service. Every payment to such an agency must have the approval of legal experts at the global headquarters and be accounted for explicitly.

EXTORTION. Politicians and bureaucrats in India sometimes seek to extract money by making wrongful but credible threats. Ambiguous and arcane laws, officials with discretionary powers, and an inefficient judiciary have created a system that is perfect for extortion. For instance, according to the Indian Packaged Commodity Act, companies that use improper price labels may have their warehouses sealed and are liable for imprisonment for a second offense. Given the ambiguity in what a proper price label is, the arbitrariness of officials, and the seriousness of the consequences, many companies find it easier to pay up than be held hostage by inspectors. This is just one small example; similar gray areas exist in many areas, especially around taxation, creating possibilities for subjectivity and therefore extortion.

Sometimes, extortion can be more than a financial matter; it may threaten lives and livelihoods. A powerful local politician once threatened to start a labor problem in one of the factories of a company

I worked for unless he was paid off. His reputation and past actions suggested that the threat was credible. Such situations are defining moments. It is easy to be moralistic and righteous until one is in the middle of a real problem; there are no easy or right answers since there are multiple considerations involved, including employee safety. Country managers need judgment and courage to tackle them. It's important not to deal with the problem alone but to discuss the matter with the global CEO and general counsel. This is a situation in which having a powerful local network and an effective advisory board can be a great help. Tense as such situations may be, extortionists are often solo rogue actors without institutional backing. It is therefore usually possible to call the extortionist's bluff, which, in my experience, helps the company cultivate a reputation for honesty that acts as a shield against future demands.

SENIOR MANAGEMENT FRAUD. Both Ernst & Young and KPMG have called attention to the growing problem of fraud by senior executives of multinational companies in India. Partly that's because of the rising pressure on financial performance; the temptation to cook the books, stuff the channel with inventory, and make side agreements with customers and partners is great. Ernst & Young's 2012 Global Fraud Survey points out a particularly disturbing trend: 15 percent of CFOs around the world are willing to pay cash payments and bribes to win business, up from 9 percent the previous year.[3]

Envy and temptation caused by rising affluence and comparisons with the compensation and lifestyles of CEOs of Indian companies may be driving more senior management fraud at multinational companies in India. Says the CEO of KPMG India, "India is growing fast, and people want to become richer faster. This leads to fraud, and governance is a real challenge today." Accepting kickbacks from advertising and media partners, commissions on real estate transactions or machinery purchases, a deposit in an overseas bank on the successful acquisition or sale of a company—these are becoming more common. In 2012, a massive fraud was uncovered at Reebok India, involving allegations of channel stuffing, secret warehouses, stolen goods, rigged books, and kickbacks. They point to the damage that arises when the gamekeeper turns poacher.[4]

VENDOR KICKBACKS AND PROCUREMENT FRAUDS. Kickbacks and fraud are quite prevalent in India and manifest themselves in several ways, according to KPMG India.[5]

- *Phantom vendors or other manipulation of the vendor master file.* By creating a record in the vendor master file that directs payment to a fictitious company or a legitimate company that does not provide services to the organization, money flows to a recipient controlled by an employee or a third party in collusion with procurement personnel. Detection may be difficult because small payments fly under the radar of senior approval authorities.

- *Fictitious invoicing and inflated billing rates.* An employee may generate an invoice payable to a vendor using the latter's home address. Or a vendor that is regularly providing legitimate services may submit an invoice for services that were not provided or at rates above those agreed on.

- *Conflicts of interest.* If procurement personnel have a financial interest in the success of a supplier, their purchase decisions will be biased toward that entity to the detriment of the organization.

- *Vendor kickbacks.* Vendors may send expensive gifts to procurement personnel because of long-term relationships. Less innocently, vendors may collude with procurement staff to work around controls. Suppliers may bribe a buyer in the organization to rig bids or to purchase from them at above-market rates. They will offer bribes or kickbacks to managers to approve fictitious charges.

Inoculating the Organization

Despite the rather grim picture I have painted, years of experience in running diverse businesses in India make me an optimist when it comes to the ability of a company, particularly a multinational company, to operate ethically. First, corruption in India may have peaked and is plausibly on the decline. Second, corruption is a two-way street. It is convenient to blame greedy politicians and public officials but succumbing to corruption is a leadership choice. Companies that are determined to succeed the right way can indeed do so and there are plenty of examples of such firms. They must of course lay down clear policies, procedures with approval processes and stringent controls, regular internal audits of high-risk areas, and so on. However, these steps are necessary but insufficient. What really safeguards companies from corruption and fraud are soft factors, namely strong local leadership and a culture of compliance.

Too many foreign companies don't pay adequate attention to compliance, mainly because India contributes so little to their revenues. Companies usually allocate budgets for audits and compliance reviews in proportion to revenues, so India escapes the scrutiny it deserves. Business insignificance, combined with cultural and geographic distance, can lead to overdependence on local management, which is risky. The global headquarters must recognize that India, like China and Russia, is a high-risk country, and all the compliance functions must pay attention to the Indian organization. Companies usually underinvest in staffing compliance functions like finance, internal audit, and legal. That's penny-wise and pound-foolish behavior, given the cost of head count in India.

Having a strong finance and administration team in India is critical; the unit is usually the primary contact with bureaucracy. Administration managers who understand local laws and regulations, possess the skills to work with government officials, and can get things done without paying bribes are a blessing. It is also critical to ensure compliance with the law without taking shortcuts. Being lax or saving costs by being too clever will create vulnerabilities that will inevitably be exposed and exploited. Dodging taxes is a particularly sensitive area, as companies like Cadbury India (a unit of Kraft) have discovered. As of this writing, Cadbury India is under investigation after managers allegedly tried to use bribes to avoid paying excise duties. The reputational damage and distraction to the business are many times higher than the magnitude of the apparent evasion.[6]

Few companies are prepared to handle fraud and corruption in India. Awareness levels are low; 51 percent of respondents in a recent survey in India were unaware of the US Foreign Corrupt Practices Act, and 65 percent didn't know of the UK Bribery Act. Only 35 percent of companies take legal action against employees, and a very small number place emphasis on codes of conduct, antibribery, and ethics training, according to Ernst & Young India's 2012 Fraud Survey. That's a major risk, with the regulatory environment of corruption changing rapidly in India. In 2011, five bills—including the Lokpal Bill, the Judicial Accountability Bill, the Public Procurement Bill, and the Whistleblower Bill—were introduced in Parliament, and several laws such as the Prevention of Corruption Act and the Companies Act are being amended.

Companies need to ensure that the basics are in place. Have they instituted a formal code of conduct that every employee has to recertify annually? Is there mandatory training on compliance, with appropriate laws and regulations for customer-facing employees? Do managers insist on preapproval for discounts, gifts, travel, and entertainment expenditures and for charitable contributions, or do they routinely approve expenses after the fact? How is the company's code of conduct communicated to customers, dealers, and partners? Do customers know the entertainment and travel reimbursement policies of the company? How does the company deal with a problem? Is investigation swift and punishment decisive and fair, and made public?

The tone local leadership sets is critical. "One thing we must appreciate is that in a hierarchical culture, bribery and corruption depend largely on the tone from the top," points out a leading fraud expert. Global companies must hold their country CEOs accountable for compliance with their policies and codes of conduct as well as Indian laws. A zero-tolerance policy is vital. Few companies discuss the character of leaders during the appraisal process; hitting the numbers is paramount. However, companies must pay attention to the small things, like segregation of personal phone calls, appropriateness of business expenses, and the personal use of company assets. I have found a sense of entitlement in small things to be a predictor of bigger problems.

Reference checks are critical when hiring. I have been burned badly; in retrospect, I could have avoided so many mistakes by better and more personal due diligence. For instance, after we terminated a senior executive for channel stuffing just one year after hiring him, a distributor told us that the executive had a reputation in the industry for indulging in that practice. When we had to let go another senior leader for inappropriate conduct with female employees, it didn't come as a surprise to many in the industry.

Global companies must hold country managers and senior leaders accountable for creating the right culture in their Indian entities by walking the talk. Subroto Bagchi, an Indian CEO, who has a reputation for creating the right culture, comments:

We ask our people to persist and prevail, not take shortcuts. Whenever they get stuck, however small the matter, like a fire clearance for a building or an issue with the electricity board, our top management walks shoulder to shoulder with operating people to get things cleared, including attending meetings with government officials. The message is simple: we will work alongside you. We will not hold it against you if a project gets delayed or we lose money; do what is right, not what is convenient. Over time, people will know what is acceptable here and what's not. Social memory is many times more effective than a bunch of policies.

By contrast, in a company that had to terminate a senior manager for a major fraud, it turned out that many employees were aware of his practices. When asked why they hadn't reported their concerns despite a widely advertised whistleblower policy, they said they didn't feel safe coming forward or felt it would be futile. The company learned a lesson on how an open and inclusive culture is critical.

Coping with Uncertainty and Volatility

Every company in India, local and foreign, has to learn to cope with volatility and uncertainty. I mentioned some factors in chapter 3, such as floods, strikes, and *bandhs* (labor shutdowns). In recent years, the government has also amplified uncertainty. Car manufacturers are on edge trying to predict the policy on fuel subsidies to decide whether to build capacity for diesel or petrol engines. Telecom companies are still unsure about the rules for 2G spectrum licenses. The software industry needs a decision on whether software imports are going to be taxed as a good or a service. For tax purposes, IT services companies are seeking clarity on the definition of software exports. New tax laws, especially the draconian General Anti-Avoidance Regulations (GAAR), have created a sense of insecurity. Martin Pieters, CEO of Vodafone India, puts it succinctly: "In emerging markets like India, there are new hurdles every day. They [policymakers] can change the rules of the market as you play in it. If you don't have the stomach for that, please don't come to India."[7]

Multinational companies face added complications, as these headlines show:

"India throws eBay Chief into prison" (*The Telegraph*)

"Victory for Novartis could spell death for millions" (*The Hindu*)

"Indian State bans Coke and Pepsi" (BBC)

"Will burn any Wal-Mart store says Uma Bharti" (NDTV)

"India allows compulsory licensing of Bayer Nexavar" (*Economic Times*)

"Facebook, Google executives face jail time" (*Times of India*)

"Vodafone case: governments tax mugging comes with big risks" (*Firstpost*)

"2G blow to govt. as Supreme Court cancels 122 licenses" (*Hindu Businessline*)

"India says 'wait' to Wal-Mart" (*Forbes*)

If India wants to attract more foreign investment, the government has to make it a less uncertain and more hospitable place. At the same time, it is important to put this uncertainty and volatility in context. Almost all emerging markets are uncertain and volatile. Brazil's fuel policy is creating uncertainty, and Google's Brazil CEO was arrested in October 2012 over a freedom-of-speech controversy. In China, an increasingly strict bureaucratic approval system and growing restrictions are hindering foreign investment.[8] Recent favorite Vietnam has already lost its appeal due to corruption and bureaucracy.[9] And Indonesia's land acquisition laws make India's look streamlined by comparison.

Since India alone isn't going through a period of heightened uncertainty, volatility, and weak political leadership, companies will need to develop more skills to handle ambiguities in policy and regulation. Smart multinational companies like Samsung, JCB, and Suzuki take that in their stride, adopt a long-term perspective, and sustain their commitment through all the vicissitudes. They have developed the ability to ward off problems, to influence policy and regulation, and to roll with the punches—resilience, in a word. Indian CEOs wryly call that managing the environment. The resilient have performed better than those that, put off by instability, have adopted a cautious approach.

Developing Resilience

Foreign companies have a particularly hard time in India because of a deficit of trust. India has benefited handsomely from globalization; its IT industry, for instance, would not exist but for globalization. However, most Indians remain ambivalent about throwing open the gates to foreign companies. These fears cannot be dismissed as irrational or paranoid; the behavior of multinational companies in emerging markets has been less than exemplary. When foreign companies do their job well, they bring desperately needed investment, technology, and managerial expertise, creating jobs and building local skills and capabilities. Importantly, they create competition, drive efficiency, and give customers more choice, lower prices, and better quality. What's not to like about them?

Plenty, argue critics. If they aren't regulated and policed, multinationals are profit-seeking missiles that destroy local competition and jobs. They minimize or evade taxes, practice cultural imperialism, and change traditional food and health habits. Nearly thirty years later, Indians haven't forgotten or forgiven the environmental disaster at the Union Carbide plant in Bhopal that affected over five hundred thousand people. Activists accuse companies like Coca-Cola of depleting groundwater supplies across India. Even responsible companies like Hindustan Unilever face accusations of poor environmental practices, such as dumping mercury-contaminated glass. Pharmaceutical companies price lifesaving drugs out of the reach of millions, while biotechnology companies like Monsanto are perceived to be enslaving farmers. The list goes on. Foreign companies' practices are regarded as a new form of economic and cultural imperialism, about which Indians, who were colonized for three centuries, are sensitive. Although Indians would like to work for multinational companies and have no reservations about buying phones or TV sets from them, even educated Indians feel they are vulnerable to exploitation by foreign companies.

The irresponsible practices of a handful of companies over time have created a trust deficit, which anyone can exploit in the noisy democracy that is India. Competitors, politicians, nongovernmental organizations (NGOs), activists, the media—they can all hijack an issue for their own agenda under the guise of standing up for the common man and in the national interest. There isn't a quicker way to make the headlines than by threatening to burn a Walmart store or to boycott McDonald's.

The most critical task is for global companies to earn the trust of all their stakeholders: customers, employees, business partners, government, NGOs, and society. One company I know that overcame a chasm of suspicion and developed the resilience to thrive in India is Microsoft.

How Microsoft India Bounced Back

"Microsoft *is* the digital divide," said India's IT minister, shortly after announcing the launch of a new low-cost PC running Linux, not Windows. Definitely not a great start to my tenure at Microsoft in India.

In early 2005, Microsoft was at the top of its game. Google and a resurgent Apple were in the future, and the primary threat was from free, open source software, which had captured the imagination of governments. Governments were concerned about Microsoft's large market shares in software and sought a free alternative to make computing accessible to millions. As in many countries, admiration for Microsoft and Bill Gates was mixed with distrust. That had much to do with the company's legal battles with the US Department of Justice and the European Union, but there were challenges in India, too. Microsoft India had gained a reputation for aggressive business practices, unaffordable prices, and the lack of relationships. That's what we had to change.

EARNING TRUST THROUGH BETTER BUSINESS PRACTICES. Microsoft had sharp elbows in India when it came to doing business. That was particularly true about piracy. Many large Indian enterprises were underlicensed; they used more software than they had paid for. Smaller firms ran almost entirely on pirated software. Every now and then, CEOs would receive an aggressive communication or a threatening visit from an arrogant Microsoft employee.

Microsoft wasn't wrong to tackle piracy, but such engagements lacked finesse. Moreover, people felt the cost of software was egregiously high relative to the plummeting cost of hardware. That rankled in a poor country like India. The government worried about the growing digital divide: those with access to IT would do much better than those denied access to it, amplifying inequity. As the industry leader, people expected Microsoft to develop solutions to bridge the digital divide, but the company didn't seem sensitive to the issue. It was easy for leaders in business and government to see open source software as the panacea. That resulted in a wave of experimentation with Linux and Open Office, with everyone trying to reduce their dependence on Microsoft or using the threat to extract better prices from us.

Fortunately, there was greater sensitivity toward such sentiments in Microsoft's headquarters in Redmond. An increasingly philanthropic Bill Gates; Brad Smith, the thoughtful general counsel; and Craig Mundie, the chief technology officer but also a sort of secretary of state for the company, were all highly attuned and receptive to the need for change.

Microsoft decided to implement a differential pricing framework globally and particularly in India. A new public-sector pricing framework transparently linked software prices to per capita GDP. A program called Partners in Learning enabled schools to get Microsoft Office for about $2.50 a year. A version of Windows called Starter Edition for India, which sold for around $20 to OEMs, made an operating system more affordable for first-time PC users. It also made local-language versions of Office available at attractive prices, to which India's state governments warmed.

To correct the perception that Microsoft Office in India cost $300, the company launched cheaper products for consumers and small businesses—products like Office Home and Student for around $70, and Windows Small Business Server—and made them available everywhere. Start-ups, student developers, and qualifying NGOs enjoyed access to the full suite of Microsoft software free through an imaginative program called Dreamspark. These efforts dramatically reduced the level of dissonance in the ecosystem. While the pricing issue never went away, perceptions of Microsoft as being unresponsive steadily changed.

Concurrently, as part of a global mission called Unlimited Potential, Microsoft launched another set of initiatives to bridge the digital divide by increasing the use of computers in India by the less affluent. Microsoft invested over $20 million to provide computer literacy to nearly 700,000 schoolteachers, who have trained almost 32 million schoolchildren and large numbers of retiring soldiers and policemen and their children. With another initiative called Saksham, Microsoft entered into a partnership with the government, NGOs, and private-sector partners to create computer kiosks in 100,000 Indian villages. These programs enabled productive partnerships with key state governments in an increasingly federal country.[10]

WINNING FRIENDS AND POLICY INFLUENCE. One memorable conversation I had when I was Microsoft India's CEO was with Deepak Pathak, a professor of computer sciences at IIT Bombay, my alma mater. An ardent supporter of open source software, Pathak was forthright in his criticism of Microsoft, but since I was a former student, tempered it with advice. Most of his advice had to do with building bridges. Microsoft stood alone ("I, me, and myself," was how Pathak characterized us), and came across as arrogant and made no friends. I vowed to change that.

It's tough to engage key stakeholders in ways that don't come across as pure self-interest. The intersection between self-interest and the national interest turned out to be policies that would increase the usage of information and communications technologies, and bridge the digital divide. Embedded in this were knotty issues such as the protection of IP rights, technology neutrality in place of a bias toward open source software, the government's use of IT, and e-governance.

The traditional approach to tackling policy issues in India is lobbying. However, those who are in charge of policy and those who influence it are cynical. They are more appreciative of companies that have developed broad national and industry viewpoints rather than narrow company-specific agendas. They expected thought leadership and the ability to bring global expertise and experience from companies like Microsoft. Microsoft India therefore invested in building the capability for thought leadership on issues important to us. We created senior roles—a national technology officer, a chief security adviser, an expert on standards, a cell comprising experts on intellectual property, and a corporate affairs team—to develop the capability to engage with industry bodies and the government. We framed issues around what is good for India and Indian industry, providing global evidence for our point of view, bringing in subject-matter experts from around the world, and creating coalitions for viewpoint. The approach proved to be effective.

Microsoft invested in creating an ecosystem of people and organizations that had a stake in developing a healthy policy environment. It ramped up engagement with India's industry associations, like NASSCOM, FICCI, and CII, in which we chaired influential committees on issues like intellectual property rights, technology and education, and software taxation. Realizing that Indian companies like Tata, Infosys, and Wipro had more credibility and influence than did foreign companies, we forged alignment with those firms on policy issues.

India's civil society, consisting of over 3 million NGOs, is an important voice. Most NGOs tend to be skeptical about the motivations of big business, especially multinationals like Microsoft. Through a program called Jyoti, Microsoft collaborated with NGOs to support initiatives to empower unemployed youth, marginalized women, farmers, fisherwomen, victims of human trafficking, and rural self-help groups by providing computer literacy and free access to computers through community centers. Between 2004 and 2011, Microsoft invested about $10 million in this program, training 430,000 people in 1,425 community technology learning centers across 27 states.[11]

Microsoft Research India (MSR), set up in Bangalore in 2005, became a platform for collaboration with top academic institutions and leading computer scientists to advance the state of computer science in India. MSR earned trust and goodwill in two ways. It focused on the burning challenge of fostering more doctoral candidates in computer science, who had numbered only a paltry thirty-five a year at that time. MSR offered internships and fellowships, provided travel grants, and ran summer schools to encourage more computer scientists to complete their degrees and pursue careers in teaching and research. By creating a new discipline called Technology for Emerging Markets, MSR India became the hub of a global community of researchers exploring challenges such as machine translation, natural interfaces, and the application of cheap mobile phones and low-cost computing to social problems. Over time, academics and researchers in India, traditionally supporters of open source software, became more balanced in their opinions about Microsoft.

Another vital decision that Microsoft India made was to engage with state governments, and not just the central government. As the central government in India weakens in authority, the action is rapidly shifting to the states. That's a positive development. As in China, leaders of many states realize that development is good politics and are vying with each other to attract investment. Their ministers and bureaucrats were keen to work with Microsoft for computer literacy, skills development, and e-governance. When decision making slowed in Delhi, Microsoft was able to make significant progress in fifteen of thirty states. Even in Kerala, where a Marxist government wasn't too keen about Microsoft, tenacious engagement paid off. Mission critical e-government applications, such as an HR management system, a road transport application, and the flagship Information Kerala Mission, were built on Microsoft technology.

One of the most sensible decisions we made was to create an advisory board for the company comprised of ten thoughtful and influential leaders drawn from diverse fields. Between 2006 and 2010, this board met three times a year with senior executives from Microsoft headquarters in Redmond. It advised the company on many specific issues, but was more helpful in educating Microsoft's senior leaders on how to do business in India. Its views were instrumental in softening the approach to India. In turn, the members developed an insider's perspective about Microsoft that they carried with them into India Inc.'s sanctum sanctorum, to which no multinational company usually has access.

MANAGING REPUTATION. The third plank of Microsoft's turnaround involved a shift away from the traditional PR approach, which was tactical and reactive. A new senior executive drove an integrated communications strategy. No longer did we define success in terms of the number of media stories about Microsoft or its share of voice. We focused on a few key messages—"Innovation in India," "Good for India," and India's need to move from renting IQ to creating IP, for instance—and told our stories around these themes.

We leveraged all of Microsoft's assets in India—Microsoft Research, the India Development Center, thousands of Microsoft partners, and the 1.2 million strong developer ecosystem—to tell these stories. Around each key theme, we ran a 360-degree campaign. We would commission research; have credible academics or analysts write white papers; engage trade associations and organize industry roundtables on the issue; send out newsletters and mailers; and write bylined articles in newspapers and magazines. To amplify the effect, we synchronized the marketing campaigns with the communications campaigns. Wherever possible, we tried to make our messages more credible through the endorsement of academics, analysts, and industry leaders. We sustained each campaign for two years, which resulted in messages becoming sticky.

The results were impressive. The Indian government's favorability toward Microsoft, measured through the International Government Elites Survey, went through the roof, with net favorability surging from the fifties to the nineties on a scale of one hundred, well ahead of Google and IBM. Microsoft was consistently recognized as one of the best Indian employers and one of the most respected multinationals in India. The aura turned the company's reputation from a headwind to a tailwind for sales teams. Indeed, greater trust, more goodwill, and a web of relationships enabled Microsoft to navigate several challenges, such as a bruising disagreement with the Indian tax authorities, a confrontation with IBM on the issue of document standards, and many attempts by the open source community to get educational institutions and local governments to ban the use of Microsoft software.

The government of India, recognizing the importance of intellectual property rights for the IT industry, increased enforcement, and the piracy rate dipped from 75 percent to 64 percent in seven years. The debate on open source versus commercial software evolved into a pragmatic acceptance of mixed source, with a focus on interoperability. The central government maintained its policy of technology neutrality, while many state governments embraced Microsoft. In fact, Microsoft's government business grew at double-digit rates over the period. Earning trust and respect turned out to be good business.

The Principles of Resilience

Based on Microsoft's experience, companies need to do a few key things in order to develop resilience.

MAKE RESILIENCE AN EXPLICIT PRIORITY. Not all companies hold the country manager in India responsible for cultivating the company's reputation, for developing relationships with influential stakeholders, and for driving thought leadership on industry issues. They should. In mature markets, that might seem less of a priority than delivering the numbers, but in India, it is central to success, especially for businesses that sell to consumers. A strong brand among employees and an image as a responsible industry leader create a favorable environment in which the business can flourish.

This has to be an organizational commitment, not just one individual's passion. What mattered at Microsoft India was not just my commitment, but that of twenty-five or more leaders across the company who represented Microsoft on industry committees, developed and sustained key relationships, and projected thought leadership.

Eventually, nearly half our employees were involved, volunteering with NGOs, engaging with software developer communities, blogging, and so on. Microsoft's willingness to sustain significant investments in public affairs capability and social programs year after year changed the company's character. Tenacity also made a difference. There were moments when a particular battle seemed irretrievably lost, but we stayed engaged. A year, sometimes two or three, later, our patience would be rewarded. A window of opportunity would open, we would make progress, and the tide would turn.

DON'T BE EVIL. The phrase, made famous by Google, isn't obvious, because evil lies in the eye of the beholder. A company may intentionally do bad things, such as dumping banned pesticides or toxic waste in an emerging market like India, taking advantage of ignorance, corruption, and weak enforcement. More often, managers merely replicate global practices or adopt a profit-maximizing approach without understanding local concerns and sentiments. That is perceived as evil, and the backlash often surprises executives.

It's important to improve business practices proactively and wholeheartedly, not reluctantly, grudgingly, and belatedly. For example, responding to criticism and protests, Coca-Cola India has focused its efforts on water conservation. It claims to have reduced water consumption by 25 percent between 2004 and 2009; that the water discharged from plants is clean enough to support aquatic life; and that Coca-Cola is supporting rainwater harvesting that replenishes 93 percent of the groundwater used. It's been a while since the company has been targeted in India.

Some pharmaceutical majors like GSK and Novartis have taken a multipronged approach to align business practices in India. Novartis, for instance, runs a large, branded generics business in its Sandoz division. Responding to criticism of the price of its cancer drug, Glivec, it manages a program that supplies Glivec priced according to patient incomes. In fact, Novartis and GSK are increasingly following a tiered pricing approach, where affluent countries like the United States pay the highest prices for a drug, and they sell them at large discounts in emerging markets like India and China. These companies now find India to be less hostile.

DO GOOD. Doing no evil is a low bar for a global company; it is imperative to do good and to be seen as good for the country. In inequitable India, where millions live in abject poverty, the expectation is that companies will give back to society. In fact, there is a movement to mandate corporate social responsibility in the Indian Companies Act. The bar is even higher for foreign companies, as I pointed out earlier.

Many multinational companies have implemented some corporate social responsibility (CSR) initiatives. The best initiatives align with the core business so synergies make the programs sustainable and scalable despite changes of leadership and fortunes. For example, Nestlé has invested heavily to help Indian milk farmers. According to the company, it has financed over 400 wells to help farmers irrigate their land for growing fodder, installed 785 cooling tanks, and 546 milking machines, and set up 3,269 milk-collection centers at a cost of Rs. 550 million (over $10 million). Nestlé also provides farmers with the services of 36 veterinary doctors and agronomists and distributes sizable quantities of fodder seeds, cattle feed, and veterinary medicines free. No wonder dairy farmers look up to Nestlé, and the company has created a capable supply chain.

CSR programs have several shortcomings. Many are anemic; companies do the bare minimum to claim the program's existence. Others have no strategy. They spread a little money across many claims, so waste it or give it to organizations that are inefficient or unaccountable. Sometimes, good intentions are tinged with arrogance. Company volunteers will show up to build toilets or schools in a village without consulting the local population, rendering such efforts a waste.

The future lies in going beyond CSR to corporate social purpose and creating shared value, as Michael Porter termed it.[12] Emily Harrison, founder of Innovaid Advisory Services, a Mumbai-based company that advises businesses on CSR, adds: "CSR is changing, moving away from corporate philanthropy and writing checks to businesses systematically managing how they affect the environment, customers, suppliers, and employees."

To improve its rural reach and be seen as a socially responsible company, Novartis India runs an innovative for-profit initiative called *Arogya Parivar* (Healthy Family, in Hindi) that delivers medicines to 40 million people at the bottom of the pyramid in ten states. The product portfolio has grown to cover eleven therapeutic areas and offers nearly eighty pharmaceutical, generic, and over-the-counter products as well as vaccines. Around 10 percent of Novartis's revenues in India come from this channel. Meanwhile, the Novartis Foundation provides free leprosy medicines in India, which has the largest leprosy population in the world. The Novartis Institute for Tropical Diseases in Singapore is working on vaccines for malaria, TB, and dengue, which the company will supply at zero profit. These measures are helping Novartis improve trust, earn goodwill, and grow in India.

Most companies check the boxes: they comply with the laws of the land, set up a foundation that runs CSR programs and funds NGOs, support educational institutions, and so on. Yet they fail to gain trust and goodwill; people remain cynical about their intentions. "There is a real risk in India that CSR just creates a new kind of patronage network, where one politician runs an educational trust, or another politician wants something done in their constituency. The risks could equally flow the other way, with companies using charitable arms to buy off opposition in local communities," says Pratap Bhanu Mehta, president of the Centre for Policy Research, a think tank in Delhi. Social activist Arundhati Roy goes further in a *Financial Times* article: "Corporations have their own sly strategy to deal with dissent. With a minuscule percentage of their profits, they run hospitals, educational institutes and trusts, which in turn fund NGOs, academics, journalists, artists, filmmakers, literary festivals and even protest movements. It is a way of using charity to lure opinion-makers into their sphere of influence. From here, it's a quick, easy step to 'there is no alternative.'"[13]

She may sound cynical, but Roy voices the views of many Indians who feel that businesses, especially multinational companies, remain self-serving. "How does one silence the skepticism?" I asked Ashok Ganguly, former chairperson of Hindustan Unilever and a respected elder statesman. Ganguly talked about the unwritten philosophy that has guided Unilever in India: What's good for India will be good for Unilever. That has been the credo of every chairperson since India's independence, and as he recounted sixty-five years of history, the extraordinary lengths to which Hindustan Unilever went to support national interests became clear.

Until quite recently, the company was called Hindustan Lever, not Unilever India, in recognition of the national pride of a newly independent nation. In the 1970s, when foreign exchange was scarce, HUL established an R&D center to drive the import substitution of oils and other raw materials, and started exporting rice, leather, and carpets—businesses that Unilever had never entered, but started up to earn foreign exchange for India. When the government wanted companies to create high-technology businesses, HUL invested in fine chemicals and catalysts. Similarly, when jobs were needed in economically backward regions, the company invested in factories in those areas despite the challenges. Since the government is now concerned about inclusive economic development, HUL has spun a pilot program under which its Shakti rural distribution network will help banks distribute financial products in rural areas.

The essential difference at companies like HUL and Tata Group is that their commitment to India is not at the margin of what these companies do, but at the core. It's not fleeting, but is sustained over decades. Moreover, these actions aren't driven by a superficial desire to look good, but by the conviction and character of its leaders. That's what gives these multinational companies the status of trusted insiders in India.

THE TAKEAWAYS

- Despite corruption in India being extraordinarily high and pervasive, it is still largely possible to operate without being corrupt and having to bribe. It takes conviction and serious focus from the top. Effective policies and controls are of course essential, but it takes more. It takes investments to prevent fraud and corruption rather than detection, investigation, and correction. Companies must also pay much more attention to soft issues: the behavior of senior leaders, a culture of high employee engagement, and the character of new hires and promoted employees.

- Another challenge is dealing with chaos and uncertainty. This is a big challenge for foreign companies because there is a trust deficit for multinationals. Multinationals also lack the capabilities to deal with the turbulent environment.

- To develop the resilience to operate in India and similar markets, the first step is to make the country manager and senior leaders explicitly accountable for the image, reputation, and influence of the company in India. The second is to change practices that cause mistrust or anger. The third step is to embrace a philosophy of doing well by doing good so that over time, the company is seen as benevolent, trustworthy, and good for India.

9

Leading the
Paradigm Shift

You can't find new land with an old map."

—PROFESSOR C. K. PRAHALAD

Vince Forlenza, chairperson and CEO of New Jersey–based medical devices manufacturer Becton Dickinson (BD), was thinking about his recent review of the company's India business with his executive team and BD India's country manager Manoj Gopalakrishnan. Since 1998, the India team had built a capable organization and a powerful brand, and delivered good financial results. Bullish about growth, the India team had proposed a strategy that in five years would make India one of BD's five biggest markets and contribute nearly 15 percent of BD's global growth over the period. Faced with headwinds in the United States and Europe, that was exactly the kind of bold thinking Forlenza had been looking for.

While the India team's ideas were reasonable, the strategy would not be easy to execute. It required not just additional investments, but also greater collaboration between New Jersey and Delhi to develop new products and solutions, partnerships, distribution channels, and novel business models. Because it would require a rebalancing of the decision rights between the product groups and geographic sales units, the strategy would require the greater engagement of Forlenza and his top team. Although he had always been bullish about India, Forlenza was worried by what he had recently seen there: slowing growth, rising corruption, and ineffective government. He wondered whether this was really the time to go big in India.

Forlenza's dilemma isn't unique; many multinational CEOs and their senior executive teams face a similar challenge. As they absorb proposals to grow their businesses in India more aggressively, fundamental questions will bubble up. To reduce costs, the India team wishes to manufacture some products locally. However, there's concern about Indian vendors' capabilities, product quality, and the impact on the brand. Besides, won't this affect jobs in US plants? The India team is also asking for an engineering center that will develop new products, but the company has just set up an R&D center in China. How many research centers can the company manage globally? Won't creating market-specific products increase proliferation and the complexity of running the business? The India team also wants to develop a low-cost product that will provide 80 percent of current functionality at less than half the cost. Even if that were possible, wouldn't such a product cannibalize sales, not just in India but also in developed markets?

The CFO will worry about how to prioritize the India investments when revenues and margins are under pressure. How is the company going to fund the 250 new positions in India that the plan demands, not to mention the additional $50 million investment? Since there is a companywide hiring freeze, it will have to trim head count in developed markets to fund growth in India. The general counsel will be concerned about corruption and protecting IP. The heads of the product divisions will wonder what all this will mean in terms of accountability. Who will have responsibility for investments, pricing, and marketing strategies? Can the India organization add people unilaterally? What if other country organizations want to operate the same way? Will we not lose economies of scale? Where will headquarters draw the line?

These are not trivial concerns but since companies lack processes and forums to debate and resolve such issues, they frequently default to maintaining the status quo. While no one will say "no" to the new India plan, nobody with authority will say "yes." With the Indian operation contributing just 1 percent to global revenues, executives at headquarters will become preoccupied with bigger and more urgent issues. As time passes, everyone will settle down to doing business as usual. If nothing changes, the initiative is lost to a competitor unless all competitors are similarly paralyzed.

Globalization Is a Paradigm Shift

While researching this book, I kept asking: Why is it so hard for CEOs to change the way multinational companies operate so they can succeed in emerging markets? Smart, accomplished, and driven executives who travel all over the world lead these companies. They regularly read publications like the *Wall Street Journal*, *The Economist*, and *Harvard Business Review*, and are well informed about what's happening in the world of business. They have access to sharp management consultants and know smart people worldwide. Why then do they struggle to comprehend that there is so much at stake for their companies' futures in India as well as in other emerging markets?

The answer finally dawned on me. What is going on is no ordinary change. This isn't just about winning in India; India is a huge market in its own right, but more importantly, it is a lead case for emerging markets. Thus, winning in India and China is actually shorthand for succeeding in the world's emerging markets. That requires not incremental evolution, but a paradigm shift.

Globalization has been happening for centuries. In the first phase, from 1492 to 1900, while companies stayed at home, countries—like

Great Britain, Spain, and France—colonized the world. In the second stage, which began around the turn of the last century and accelerated after World War II, Western and Japanese companies ventured overseas. They started in other developed countries but gradually established a presence in some developing countries, too. The model they used was an export-oriented model, or, as C. K. Prahalad said more bluntly, an imperialist mind-set.[1] Emerging markets provided incremental sales for existing products, usually older or obsolescent ones, and international companies focused only on the affluent because they were the only consumers who could afford them. Decision making was centralized at headquarters, which was seen as the locus of innovation for products, business models, and management practices, and was the hub of the smartest people in the organization. This is still the dominant model and as a result, says one CEO, "multimillion-dollar thinking routinely obscures a multibillion-dollar opportunity in these markets."

The next wave of globalization will be qualitatively different. With markets in the developed countries saturated and competitive, and with many of those economies slowing down, growth tomorrow will have to come from emerging markets. The center is rapidly shifting from the West; growth will come mainly from the rapidly growing middle class in the developing countries. However, most companies' current business models do not address them effectively. To do well in emerging markets, global companies will have to learn to do things differently. For instance, most multinational companies' models allocate resources and investments based on their current revenues in each market. That has to be tempered by a judgment about the size of the potential opportunity, and companies have to make differentiated bets on specific countries such as India, China, and Brazil.

Current business models assume homogeneity of markets and customer needs, but that's no longer true. One size no longer fits everyone, and local innovation is critical. Success requires different, and more affordable, value propositions, which companies can only develop in local markets. The current model assumes the world is familiar and predictable; therefore, headquarters can decide and subsidiaries execute. Emerging markets are different terrain; they're unfamiliar, uncertain, and culturally dissimilar. You cannot succeed in these places unless you have a local team you can trust to make the right decisions. Many developing countries are traumatized by their colonial pasts, distrustful of foreign companies, and worried about a new kind of economic imperialism. Corporations have to operate more sensitively and inclusively, and deploy sustainable business practices to earn trust and avoid a backlash.

Most multinational companies can be characterized as centralized hub-and-spoke systems, with headquarters in the center. They need a new architecture, with multiple hubs in India, China, and other countries. These hubs will have global missions, not just national ones, and evenly distributed decision-making power. For instance, the Indian hub's mission will be to develop innovative products and solutions for the middle of the pyramid, nurture leaders who can operate in chaotic emerging markets, and become the back office for IT, engineering, and business processes.

Leading such a hub is very different from heading a sales subsidiary. The process cannot be delegated to enthusiastic middle-level managers who approach everything from the India perspective. It requires an entrepreneurial general manager with a global perspective, one who can make judgment calls about balancing global objectives with local needs. While the hubs will have more authority, they still cannot make unilateral decisions, which will require a new operating framework. That isn't likely to be a tweaking of the current approach, but a profound shift in mind-set, architecture, operating model, capabilities, and, most of all, power. It will feel unfamiliar, threatening, and disruptive. That's why it represents a paradigm shift.

The CEO's Role

Because it is a paradigm shift, the globalization of corporations will run into resistance internally. For instance, in an interview with the *Economic Times* in 2009, GE's Jeff Immelt candidly admitted that the reaction of his executives in India to the One GE model had been less than positive. "The only person who believes that it's a good idea is me," he joked.[2] To have a chance of success, the CEO, supported by the company's board, has to champion change. Driving the changes in the globalization model shouldn't be delegated to the international president or the global sales head, no matter how capable the individual. Globalization requires the whole company to change, not just one of its parts. Product divisions, functions like finance and HR, and most of the core processes of the company have to be part of the transformation. Only the CEO can drive that kind of change.

That poses a problem because few CEOs understand, let alone focus on, emerging markets. When IBM conducted a survey of fifteen hundred CEOs in 2010, it found that most CEOs don't fully comprehend the implications and certainly aren't preparing their companies for them.[3] While 76 percent of CEOs see a major shift of economic power from the West to developing markets, only 23 percent believe that globalization will have a big impact on their organizations in the next five years. While many Western CEOs claim that 50 percent to 60 percent of their future growth will come from emerging economies like India and China, they admit that only 2 percent of senior leadership has work experience in those regions. Thus, ninety-eight of a hundred senior executives in *Fortune* 500 firms are likely defending business models created in the United States and Europe that may not have much relevance in emerging markets.

During my conversations with CEOs and senior corporate leaders in the West, it became apparent that many lack a visceral understanding of emerging markets like India. Their understanding is academic, gleaned from presentations, spreadsheets, books, quick visits, and vacations. Many have no real liking for places like India or Indonesia, which they see as alien, chaotic, and difficult to manage. They find it hard to imagine that India could have the same GDP as Germany does in their lifetimes.

These CEOs are also more focused on the short term. With a Western CEO's average tenure at around six years, few have the patience to build a presence in places like India, which may take ten years. Only a rare CEO is willing to take on the risks and challenges of building market leadership in emerging markets, knowing that history will credit success, if it comes, to a successor. It is simpler to drive revenues and margin growth from existing businesses and geographies.

Besides, the complexity of the environment is rising sharply. Markets are more challenging, competition is tougher, and governments are intervening more, so a large number of issues clamor for the CEO's attention. Only a few will prioritize their agenda in emerging markets, especially when countries like Russia and India aren't presenting themselves as great places for multinational companies to do business. Few CEOs have globalization as one of their top-three priorities.

The Globalizers

There are always exceptions. A small number of CEOs, convinced that globalization is a disruptive opportunity, are making the shift hands-on. Sam Palmisano moved IBM's center of gravity to India for services and to China for manufacturing; IBM has more employees in India than in the United States. Tim Solso drove the transformation of Cummins India and China into hubs that generate nearly half the company's profits. Leif Johansson has grown Volvo's Asia operations from 5 percent to 35 percent of global revenues. Schneider Electric's Jean-Pascal Tricoire has relocated himself and a third of his executive team to Hong Kong to be close to China and India. Others, such as Honeywell's Dave Cote, Deere's Sam Allen, and GE's Jeff Immelt, are relentlessly remaking their companies so they become more competitive in emerging markets.

I call these CEOs *globalizers*. They represent a distinct kind of business leader, different from other archetypes, such as the cost cutters; the generals who obsess about execution; the salespersons, who love being with customers; and the engineers who are passionate about shaping products. Globalizers have an overarching desire to create a global enterprise and to be leaders in growth markets. These CEOs don't underestimate the magnitude of the challenge in getting their companies to be more attuned to emerging markets. Globalizers are masters of change management. Rather than trying to change the whole company, they use India and China as laboratories to cook new models for other emerging markets. Given the relatively tiny revenues that most companies get from India, it's a low-risk, high-reward experiment.

Globalizers use several strategies to drive their agenda. They invite the country heads of China and India to key leadership meetings so that these strategic hubs have a seat at the executive table. They create alignment and accountability by giving business unit heads explicit targets for key geographic areas. Performance in China and India isn't just the responsibility of the president of sales or international markets, and division presidents won't be rewarded for hitting their financial numbers if they miss their goals for key countries. Honeywell's Cote holds himself personally accountable by breaking out the numbers for China and India and talking about them in every earnings call. He has also encouraged senior leaders to operate out of China and India. Thus, Krishna Mikkileni, Honeywell's global leader for manufacturing and engineering, operates from Bangalore, while Shane Tedjarati, president for high-growth markets, operates out of China. Wearing dual hats—a global role and a country responsibility—is an effective way of advancing globalization.

Smart CEOs manage strategic geographies like China and India the same way they manage product divisions. Like SBUs, these countries are profit centers managed with multiyear plans, not just annual budgets. The CEOs review, debate, and refresh the strategies for these countries every year as part of the planning process. That allows the CEOs to surface and resolve contentious issues right away.

Like JCB's Anthony Bamford, globalizers actively shape the company culture to facilitate globalization. They recognize that an inward-looking or ethnocentric culture, a large headquarters staff, hierarchy, and silos are all enemies of globalization. They actively encourage learning and collaboration and discourage talking down to the geographic subsidiaries.

Globalizers are adept at using forcing functions to overcome resistance. IBM's transformational outsourcing deal with telecom operator Bharti got many parts of the company engaged with it, and it has become a fast-growing line for the company. Cummins's Solso and Volvo's Johansson have used joint ventures in China and India to change the way their companies think. Cisco's John Chambers created Cisco East, an R&D center in Bangalore to decentralize both innovation and the location of 20 percent of Cisco's senior leaders. Giving the India team the responsibility for a product line can be effective. Deere's decision to use India as an export base has made it more competitive in the small-tractor segment worldwide.

Globalizers are deeply involved with developing the leadership bench in countries like India and China. Ensuring that talent flows across the system, they personally tap rising stars to take on roles in markets like India. They get involved in recruiting the right country head and remain accessible to mentor him or her. At Renault, Carlos Ghosn has given his India president, Marc Nassif, permission to put knotty issues on the agenda of the executive committee. That power ensures that most issues get resolved without having to be escalated. Nokia's D. Shivakumar has a standing invitation to meet with CEO Stephen Elop informally during every visit to Finland. Nestlé's Helio Waszyk doesn't wait for an invitation; he simply drops into CEO Paul Bulcke's office whenever the latter is in town, for an informal chat about the India business. Such informal access is crucial for mentoring and for the CEO to tear down internal barriers quickly.

Globalizers understand the importance of reverse innovation. They get personally involved with ideas and experiments in developing countries, looking for promising ideas and for lessons from failed experiments. When promising innovations fail to scale, the CEO's involvement ensures that they aren't forgotten. GE, for instance, has done an impressive job with low-cost X-ray and ultrasound machines from China and India, but they haven't been game changers. However, CEO Immelt has publicly made a big deal of these innovations, including coauthoring a widely read article in *Harvard Business Review*.[4] That makes it hard for GE Healthcare to give up. Learning from the initially disappointing results, GE executives have realized that they need more marketing investments to create a strong brand, a different sales strategy, and global distribution.

Globalizers ask what new business the company could be in if it were headquartered in India or China. In emerging markets, many companies may find themselves confronted by new opportunities that they are well positioned to address. For instance, when I headed Cummins India in 1999, we felt we should be in the software business. We designed a creative deal with a small IT company, and as a result, Cummins is a major shareholder in one of India's fastest-growing IT companies, KPIT Cummins Infosystems, a leader in embedded software, among other things. Globalizers continuously question people on the front lines as well as folks at the center to understand if new segments have opened up because of innovations. That's how Solso learned about Cummins India's small generator sets business and ensured that it became a global business for its parent.

At a personal level, globalizers tend to be open, curious, and adventurous. For instance, they enjoy eating ethnic food in nondescript restaurants in the countries they visit rather than bringing familiar food on their company jets or staying in the safe confines of fancy hotels. They have friends in China, India, and Turkey, not just business associates. They enjoy taking vacations in different countries and are likely to be excited by the traffic rather than getting frustrated, worried, or wishing they were back home.

Globalizers enjoy wallowing in overseas markets to develop a visceral understanding of the opportunities and challenges. Nokia's Elop insists on spending day one of a country visit in the market, with no internal meetings. Tricoire has ridden a motorcycle across the Indian countryside to understand how people live and how retail stores and distribution networks work. Deere's Allen spent a week doing community service in a small village in Rajasthan with a number of senior executives. This contrasts sharply with the CEO fly-by—the annual daylong stop of the company jet in Delhi.

Such CEOs are invariably inclusive leaders with a passion for diversity. To them, diversity is a lot more than the percentages of women or people of color working for them. They are passionate about creating a culture that is blind to color, passports, gender, ethnicity, or language. They are open to ideas from everywhere, engaging with shop-floor workers and eating with employees in company canteens. Like magnets, they are drawn to the energy and ideas of employees, especially young stars.

Globalizers use intuition and judgment to make decisions, not just analysis and data. As the saying goes, they rely on their heads, hearts, and guts. Three CEOs expressed the same idea while explaining why they invested early in India. Said Volvo's Johansson: "If you wait till a trend is obvious, it's too late. I saw in India a country with a billion people and many smart managers, and asked how we could be global if we were not leaders in this market." JCB's Bamford stated: "The engineering talent and the people I met impressed me. I saw a country with no infrastructure and knew it would simply be a matter of time." Echoed Solso: "I felt the country stirring and sensed that things could take off." Their intuition comes from engaging personally with the market, not by sitting in a boardroom looking at presentations and asking for more analysis and data. Harvard professor Clay Christensen explains why it is so hard for senior managers to spot and respond quickly to a threat or opportunity: "A fundamental problem about the world is that data is only available about the past. If you wait until the data is clear, you're going to be taking action when the game is over."[5] Neither data nor analysis could have predicted the success of Facebook or Apple; you had to feel their potential emotionally and viscerally. Similarly, no amount of data will serve as an indicator of a market's rise. That is a judgment call.

Many of these CEOs also have a passion for creating social value, not just shareholder value. Like Solso, they are passionate about creating workplaces that unleash the potential of people or, like Johansson, want to see more people have access to clean and safe trucks and buses. These leaders have an almost evangelical belief that extending their business to more markets will quietly make the world a better place.

Boards and Globalization

Most boards are passive when it comes to globalization. This is likely to have serious long-term consequences; these companies will likely cede leadership to competitors that are rapidly building leadership in emerging markets like India. Apple's de facto decision to abdicate difficult markets like India to Samsung, Nokia, and Huawei will have consequences in the future.[6]

Given what is at stake, boards have a fiduciary responsibility for companies' strategy and performance in emerging markets. They should ask themselves and CEOs:

- How often do we discuss the company's performance and strategy in key emerging markets like India? Does the board know how well competitors are doing in these markets?

- Does the CEO have explicit goals for key emerging markets like China and India? Is it right for leaders to ignore emerging markets as long as they hit their overall targets?

- Is the CEO a globalizer? Should this be a key criterion in our choice of successor?

- Is it important that the board have members from key emerging markets?

- Should the company have board meetings in emerging markets? How often does the executive team hold meetings in these markets?

- How global is the company's executive leadership team? How many live outside the home country? How many are located in China and India? Should we have goals for what we want in five years?

Winning in India is not just about India; it is a metaphor for winning in emerging markets. The Indian market is big, but fundamentally it is a litmus test for the ability to adapt, compete, and innovate in emerging markets. You have to be able to win in India today if you wish to win anywhere else in the world tomorrow.

THE TAKEAWAYS

- The next wave of globalization, anchored in the emerging middle class in Asia, Latin America, and Africa, requires companies to embrace a different paradigm, including a different mind-set, organizational architecture, and governance framework. Because this is incredibly hard for most organizations, little changes.

- Industry leadership usually changes during paradigm shifts, so globalization represents a threat to today's leaders. Smaller rivals who seize the emerging market opportunity faster or hungry new competitors from those markets are likely to supplant them.

- India is important not just as a market with large potential, but because it is at the cutting edge of the new markets. It embodies the potential and the challenges of many emerging markets and is a laboratory in which to figure out how to win in those markets.

- Because the globalization agenda takes a paradigm shift rather than incremental changes, the CEO has to take the lead and cannot delegate it. However, it takes a very different CEO to drive this agenda.

- Boards of directors have been conspicuously missing in action when it comes to globalization. Given the stakes, they need to be more diverse and more engaged with the issue, and to ensure that CEOs focus on winning in countries like China and India.

10

Win in India to Win Everywhere

Learnings from India, such as lower price points for products in smaller packages or sachets, are gaining acceptance in Europe, where poverty has returned.

—PAUL POLMAN, CHAIRMAN AND CEO, UNILEVER

My research for this book was almost done when I made a stop at Deere & Company. "Has competing in India helped Deere succeed in the rest of the world?" I asked global CFO Rajesh Kalathur and vice president Bharat Vedak. As I discussed earlier, India represents both a major opportunity and a potent threat for Deere. While India is the world's largest tractor market in units, an Indian player, Mahindra & Mahindra, has leveraged its strengths in India to challenge Deere globally in the market for small tractors. Deere's managers realized that unless they learned to compete successfully in India, they would have a challenge in many other parts of the world, including the United States. The Indian market thus became the front line of a global battle for leadership in the small tractor segment.

Kalathur, who came to India in 2005 to establish the John Deere Technology Center India (TCI) in Pune and became the CEO of John

Deere India, led Deere's charge. "We had to learn to compete all over again," he says. Engineers had to understand how Indian farmers used tractors. They discovered that tractors are smaller, usually less than 50 HP, often abused, running for three times the number of hours in a year as in developed markets and at half the price of other markets. Deere realized that starting with a clean sheet design rather than simply tweaking an existing model would be important to compete effectively. The series 5000 tractor that it developed went on to become a major success; Deere has been able to quickly gain market share in India and compete effectively in the small tractor market worldwide including the USA.

According to Kalathur and Vedak, learning to compete in India has been a pivotal experience. As Kalathur said: "India is a microcosm … everything in the world is in one place." The tough price points meant that marketers and engineers had to question every feature. Something that added $5 to the cost was not a big deal to an engineer in Waterloo, Iowa, used to designing a $250,000 machine; however, Rs. 250 was a huge deal to frugal-minded Indian engineers. This proved to be important as tough Chinese competitors began entering the US market. Another Deere executive said, "Our experience putting a new dealer network in place helped us do this more effectively in Africa and other parts of Asia like Thailand. We had to relearn marketing; for the first time, our deep institutional knowledge of farmers built over generations was less relevant. We had to fundamentally understand customer requirements and build market-appropriate offerings. We had to think differently about pricing. We had to relearn how to convince farmers." The TCI has also mushroomed into the single-largest concentration of engineers in the Deere world and is now integrated into the global product development process. It has developed world-leading capabilities in areas such as factory simulation, embedded software, and analysis. "All our product lines and all our functions intersect in Pune," said Vedak.

There are also significant flows of talent between India and the rest of the world. CFO Kalathur's own story illustrates this. Starting out in the US and Mexican operations of Deere, Kalathur moved to India in 2005 to build Deere's business there. His success won him a promotion as the head of sales and marketing for China, India, South and East Asia, and Sub-Saharan and South Africa, before he finally became global CFO in 2012. According to Vedak and Kalathur, the connection between India and Africa is particularly significant. With a large India diaspora in many parts of Africa, many Indian teachers in Africa, and English as a common language, Africans are predisposed to working with Indians. The rugged inexpensive and reliable products from India work well on African farms. This makes India a natural hub for supplying products as well as for managing functions like marketing and even HR. Concluded Kalathur: "We are still quite early in the journey, but India's contribution to our success worldwide is palpable. Most of all, it has made us more flexible, more open to different approaches and market-appropriate products and ultimately more competitive." The fiercely contested tractor market in India has clearly helped reignite Deere's competitive spirit.

Deere's experience is playing out in many companies, which are discovering that globalization is very much a two-way street. When a company enters India, it carefully shapes the new subsidiary in its own mold. It faithfully replicates systems, processes, and policies locally, and transfers products and capabilities. Over time, as the young subsidiary matures, as it learns to compete in the all-important and difficult middle market, the company develops innovative new products, capabilities, and talent that are important in many other markets. Ultimately, these may be as important a reason that India matters to an MNC as the size of the market.

The benefits occur along five dimensions. First, India can help create a tremendous cost advantage. Many companies are successfully using India for sourcing components, products, engineering work, and IT services. What differentiates companies is the vigor with which they embrace this and the scale at which they operate. Honeywell's technology center, for instance, employs nearly thirteen thousand engineers. GE's John F. Welch Technology Centre in Bangalore is its largest technology center in the world. At Dell and IBM, a third of all employees are in India. At Cummins, India is the global hub for the high horsepower engine and small generator sets. At all these companies, Indian talent, suppliers, and manufacturing are not at the periphery of the business but an important hub in the global network because of the low production costs.

Two, India is a source of innovative new products, business models, and distinctive innovation capabilities. Authors like Vijay Govindarajan have written extensively about reverse innovation. The list of success stories is varied and growing rapidly: IBM and Ericsson's managed services for telecom operators, Ford's Figo car, and GE Healthcare's MAC range of ultrasound machines are all well-known examples. Increasingly, companies are developing not just products but innovative distribution and retail systems as well. Novartis is replicating its highly successful *Arogya Parivar* (Healthy Family) distribution program aimed at the bottom of the pyramid in several other Asian and African countries, for instance. Schneider Electric found that its acquisition of Indian company Luminous Power suddenly gave it retailing and business-to-consumer capabilities that it had nowhere else in the world. Luminous taught Schneider how Indian companies combine tax optimization, frugal engineering, and distribution reach (twenty thousand outlets) to create a model that delivers extraordinary profitability. Schneider is taking this model to fifteen countries, including Brazil.

Similarly, French cosmetics giant L'Oréal is replicating its successful Indian distribution model overseas. "We are now in different stages of moving from a few distributors in emerging countries such as the Philippines and Indonesia to several of them, similar to how we operate in India, where we have over 750 distributors serving millions of retail outlets," said a senior L'Oréal executive. The Indian units of consumer goods firms, such as Unilever, Danone, Kraft, Coca-Cola, and GlaxoSmithKline, are all taking their learning from working with small Indian grocers to other markets where their products currently sell only in a relatively few modern retail outlets.

A third source of competitive advantage is talent. Competing in India breeds talented executives who can do well globally. Smart companies create a strong flow of talent into and out of India. Consumer products (fast-moving consumer goods) companies like Unilever, Reckitt Benckiser, and L'Oréal in particular have been very proactive in using talented managers from India in other markets. India is globally the best-performing unit for Volvo Bus; as a result, Akash Passey, who built this business, has been promoted to oversee growth in all emerging markets, including China, Asia, Oceania, the Middle East, and Africa. As *Time* flatly stated:

> India's Leading Export? CEOs. Competitive and complex, India is the perfect petri dish in which to grow a 21st century CEO ... Multiculturalism? Check. Complex competitive environment? Check. Resource-constrained developing economy? You got that right. Indian executives think in English, they're used to multinationals in their country, they're very adaptive, and they're supremely confident. Unlike, say, a Swede or a German, an Indian executive is raised in a multiethnic, multifaith, multilingual society, one nearly as diverse as the modern global marketplace. Unlike Americans, they're well versed in negotiating India's byzantine bureaucracy, a key skill to have in emerging markets. And unlike the Chinese, they can handle the messiness of a litigious democracy.[1]

Fourth, competing successfully in emerging markets like India profoundly changes the corporate mind-set. As hundreds of executives flow back and forth over the years, companies slowly become open to ideas from elsewhere. Olof Persson of Volvo comments, "China and India have been real eye openers. The most important lesson is that you need different products/offers for different market segments and you need to do this in that market. As a result of our joint ventures with Eicher in India and Lingong in China, we have developed frugal engineering capability and more expansive thinking about using multiple brands to address different segments globally." Oliver Blum of Schneider Electric adds, "China and India have given us a growth mind-set. We are faster, more agile, and take more risk. We like to experiment rather than let too much analysis get in the way." Most of all, companies develop the confidence and capabilities to tackle other difficult markets. Tom Linebarger, chairman of Cummins, says, "Learning to work with partners in India and China made us more innovative at finding ways to make money. What we have learned is that the more difficult the market is, the more money we make, because others will struggle more, or not even enter. We are also better at assessing the real risk of these markets, which can often appear bigger than it actually is. We make less money in easier markets because everyone knows how to compete in them."

Finally, companies that succeed in making India, China, and other emerging markets into significant engines of their growth are viewed differently from their peers. As growth slows in the developed world and the economic center of the world moves inexorably toward the East, companies need to demonstrate that they have their acts together in China and India. Explained Tim Solso: "For years, even with record profits, Cummins had a lower P/E due to our cyclicality. It wasn't until the recession of 2008–2010, when India, China, and Brazil carried the company, contributing a huge part of our profits, that we broke the back of our rating as a cyclical company." Similarly, Unilever's strong performance in emerging markets led by its leadership in India has allowed it to reclaim momentum from traditional rival P&G, which has a more dominant position in slower-growing developed markets.[2]

Back to the Future

In the 1970s, resource constraints forced Japanese companies to develop the quality and lean manufacturing techniques that proved disruptive. Very few Western companies succeeded in a meaningful way in the Japanese market, and as a result, they could not compete when Japanese competitors challenged them in their home markets. A large part of the manufacturing base in Europe and the United States was overwhelmed as a result.

In the same way, winning in India becomes important not only because it is a major market but also because its unique combination of opportunities, diversity, and adversity is a catalyst for the development of powerful new capabilities that are critical for competing worldwide. Offense is also the best defense. As Deere discovered, taking on competitors in India and China in their home markets is the best way of developing antibodies. Win in India, win everywhere.

NOTES

CHAPTER 1

1. Unless otherwise cited, all quotes come from my interviews.

2. David Pilling, "India's Bumblebee Defies Gravity," *Financial Times*, February 15, 2012. For a fuller discussion of the drivers of growth for MNCs, see "Winning in India," McKinsey Asia Center, 2011.

3. "Top 10 Abuses of Power," *Time*, May 17, 2011.

4. James Crabtree, "India's Growth Threatened by Old Abuses," *Financial Times*, May 15, 2012.

5. "Decision to Amend IT Act Retrospectively 'Capricious,' Says Economist Raghuram Rajan," *Economic Times*, April 12, 2012.

6. "Act or We Could Become Banana Republic: Tata Strikes Back," *Indian Express*, November 27, 2010.

7. "The Regulator Without a Fan," *Business Today*, June 24, 2012.

8. The phrase "new Hindu rate of growth" describes decades of slow growth under socialism.

9. *The Prospect*, January 2012, http://www2.lse.ac.uk/IDEAS/publications/reports/SR010.aspx.

10. Paul Beckett, "Honeywell Warns India Is Scaring Away Foreign Investors," *Wall Street Journal*, May 3, 2012.

11. Bart Vogel and S. Barasia, "How Global Telcos Can Profit from India's Wireless Experience," Bain & Company, http://www.bain.com/Images/BBIndia_Telcos_4-11-11.pdf.

12. "We Use India to Scale Up in Africa," *Economic Times*, January 21, 2011.

13. "Dual-SIM Phones Help Beat Back Competition in India: Stephen Elop, Nokia CEO," *Economic Times*, September 8, 2011.

CHAPTER 2

1. McKinsey Asia Center, http://www.mckinsey.com/client_service/strategy/mckinsey_asia_center.

2. Peter Marsh, "Performance in Asia Crucial for Caterpillar," *Financial Times*, November 16, 2009.

3. "India Will Be the Centerpiece of Our Growth," *Forbes India*, December 2009. (Note that GE does not break out India figures and this is an estimate from industry sources; average orders for the three years post the change [2010–2012] are 55 percent higher than the three years prior to the change [2007–2009].)

4. Samar Srivastava, "Adidas versus Subhinder," *Forbes India* blog, September 21, 2012.

5. "Fighting for the Next Billion Shoppers," *The Economist*, June 30, 2012.

6. The following discussion about GE is drawn from the following sources: Jeffrey Immelt, Vijay Govindarajan, and Chris Trimble, "How GE Is Disrupting Itself," *Harvard Business Review*, October 2009; Neelima Mahajan-Bansal and Malini Goyal, "GE Has Its Finger on the Indian Pulse, at Last," *Forbes India*, December 16, 2009; Neelima Mahajan-Bansal and Malini Goyal, "GE Is Flat-Footed, Not Knowledgeable and Missing What the Local Market Needs," *Forbes India*, December 16, 2009; Neelima Mahajan-Bansal and Malini Goyal, "Jeff Immelt: 'India Will Be a Centrepiece in Our Growth,'" *Forbes India*, December 16, 2009; and Neelima Mahajan-Bansal, "I Want GE India to Be Viewed as One of India's Best Indian Companies," *Forbes India*, December 16, 2009.

7. C. K. Prahalad, "End of Corporate Imperialism," *Harvard Business Review*, August 2003.

8. For an articulation of the idea of a paradigm shift, see Thomas Kuhn, *The Structure of Scientific Revolutions* (Chicago: University of Chicago Press, 1996).

CHAPTER 3

1. For instance, see Dave Ulrich, Norm Smallwood, and Kate Sweetman, *The Leadership Code: Five Rules to Lead By* (Boston: Harvard Business Press, 2009).

2. See Nathaniel Foote, Russ Eisenstat, and Tobias Fredberg, "The Higher Ambition Leader," *Harvard Business Review*, September 2011.

3. Warren Bennis and Robert Thomas, *Geeks and Geezers: How Era, Values, and Defining Moments Shape Leaders* (Boston: Harvard Business School Press, 2002).

4. Claudio Fernández-Aráoz, *Great People Decisions: Why They Matter So Much, Why They Are So Hard, and How You Can Master Them* (New York: Wiley, 2007).

5. For more, read Tony Schwartz, with Jean Gomes and Catherine McCarthy, *Be Excellent at Anything* (New York: Free Press, 2011).

CHAPTER 4

1. For market share, see "Nokia Loses Its India Plot," *Economic Times*, September 29, 2010.

2. Mehrdad Baghai, Stephen Coley, and David White, *The Alchemy of Growth* (New York: Basic Books, 2000).

3. Sumantra Ghoshal and Chris Bartlett, *Managing Across Borders: The Transnational Solution* (Boston: Harvard Business School Press, 2002).

4. IIM Bangalore Case Study, "Bosch Group in India: Transition to a Transnational Organization," IIM Bangalore, 301.

5. Ibid.

6. The history buff should read Nick Robbins, *The Corporation That Changed the World* (London: Pluto Press, 2012); Philip Mason, *The Men Who Ruled India* (New York: Jonathon Cape Ltd, 1989); or "The Company That Ruled the Waves," *The Economist*, December 2011.

CHAPTER 5

1. "Delivering Results through Talent: The HR Challenge in a Volatile World," PwC 15th Annual CEO Survey 2012, http://www.pwc.com/gx/en/ceo-survey/key-findings/hr-talent-strategies.jhtml.

2. PwC Saratoga Human Capital Effectiveness Survey, www.pwc.com/saratoga.

3. "Best Companies to Work for in India," Indicus–*Business Today* survey, March 4, 2012, http://businesstoday.intoday.in/story/best-companies-to-work-india-survey-business-today/1/22284.html.

4. Bill Conaty and Ram Charan, *The Talent Masters: Why Smart Leaders Put People Before Numbers* (New York: Crown Business, 2010); Stephen Remedios, "Transformation—How Hindustan Unilever Makes CEOs out of College Kids," *Management Exchange*, October 10, 2012, http://www.managementexchange.com/.

5. Nitin Paranjpe, Hindustan Unilever, press release, "K.B. Dadiseth Unveils HLL's New Growth Blueprint," http://www.hul.co.in/mediacentre/pressreleases/2000/KBDadisethUnveilsHLLsNewGrowthBlueprint.aspx.

6. Ram Kumar, "Human Resource Professionals Have Lost Sight of the Connect with Their People," *Economic Times*, August 17, 2012.

7. Saumya Bhattacharya, "How We Can Love HR and What HR Must Do for That," *Economic Times*, March 11, 2012.

8. Kala Vijayraghavan and Chaitali Chakravarty, "What Ails HUL? Strategic Changes by CEO Paul Polman Upset Indian Executives," *Economic Times*, January 24, 2012.

9. Arijit Barman, "Senior MNC Execs Jump Ship as India Inc Empowers Them," *Business Standard*, February 20, 2012.

10. Nitin Nohria, "Why Globalization Will Revolutionize Talent Management," *The Focus* XI, no. 2 (2008): 24–27.

CHAPTER 6

1. See, for instance, Vijay Govindarajan and Chris Trimble, *Reverse Innovation* (Boston: Harvard Business Review Press, 2012); or Nirmalya Kumar and Phanish Puranam, *India Inside* (Boston: Harvard Business Review Press, 2011); or Navi Radjou, *Jugaad Innovation: Think Frugal, Be Flexible, Generate Breakthrough Growth* (New York: Jossey Bass, 2012).

2. See "The Fortune Just above the Bottom," *Economic Times*, March 6, 2012.

3. McKinsey Asia Center report, "How Multinationals Can Win in India," *McKinsey Quarterly*, March 2012.

4. See V. Kasturi Rangan, "Hindustan Unilever's 'Pureit' Water Purifier," case 511-067 (Boston: Harvard Business School, rev 2012).

5. See Govindarajan and Trimble, *Reverse Innovation*.

6. C. K. Prahalad, "How to Be a Truly Global Company," *Strategy+ Business*, Autumn 2011.

7. Eric Ries, *The Lean Startup: How Today's Entrepreneurs Use Continuous Innovation to Create Radically Successful Businesses* (New York: Crown Business, 2011).

8. Dell interviews; and "How Dell Conquered India," *Fortune*, February 10, 2011, http://tech.fortune.cnn.com/2011/02/10/how-dell-conquered-india/.

9. Ibid.

10. "Ratan Tata Says Nano Can Still Be Successful," *India Today*, January 6, 2012.

11. See "Microsoft Knits Windows into India," http://www.forbes.com/forbes/2008/0929/074.html.

12. Ibid.

CHAPTER 7

1. Ashish K. Mishra, "The Education of Carlos Ghosn," *Forbes India*, December 8, 2011.

2. David F. Hawkins, "Caterpillar, Inc. (A)," Case 111-031 (Boston: Harvard Business School, September 2011).

3. "Act Quickly, Execute Flawlessly," *People Matters*, July 1, 2011.

CHAPTER 8

1. See http://www.kpmg.com/in/en/issuesandinsights/articlespublications/pages/fraudsurvey12.aspx.

2. World Economic Forum, The Global Competitiveness Report 2011–2012, http://www.weforum.org/reports/global-competitiveness-report-2011-2012; Economic Intelligence Unit; Kroll, Global Fraud Report (2011–2012 annual edition), http://www.krolladvisory.com/library/KRL_FraudReport2012-13.pdf.

3. Ernst & Young, "Fraud and Corporate Governance—A Changing Paradigm in India," 2012, http://www.ey.com/IN/en/Services/Assurance/

Fraud-Investigation---Dispute-Services/Fraud-and-corporate-governance-Changing-paradigm-in-India.

4. Binoy Prabhakar and Chaitali Chakravarty, "How Adidas Slipped in India," *Economic Times*, May 13, 2012.

5. See http://www.kpmg.com/in/en/issuesandinsights/articlespublications/pages/fraudsurvey12.aspx.

6. Samar Srivastava, "Sticky Situation at Cadbury India," *Forbes India*, August 15, 2012.

7. Heather Timmons, "For Vodafone in India, a Swift but Bumpy Rise," *New York Times*, March 27, 2011.

8. See "The New Great Wall of China," *Time*, September 2012, http://www.time.com/time/magazine/article/0,9171,2124406,00.html.

9. See "From Tiger to Pussycat: How Vietnam's Economy Got Off Track," *Newsweek*, October 1, 2012.

10. Read more at http://www.microsoft.com/india/msindia/msindia_up_partnerslearning.aspx.

11. For details, see www.microsoft.com/india/msindia/msindia_ourmission_projectjyoti.aspx.

12. Michael Porter, "Creating Shared Value," *Harvard Business Review* blog, http://hbr.org/2011/01/the-big-idea-creating-shared-value.

13. Arundhati Roy, "Beware the 'Gush-Up Gospel' Behind India's Billionaires," *Financial Times*, January 13, 2012.

CHAPTER 9

1. C. K. Prahalad and Kenneth Lieberthal, *The End of Corporate Imperialism* (Boston: Harvard Business Press, 2008).

2. Himangshu Watts, "General Electric CEO: India Story Is Unfolding as Expected," *Economic Times*, September 26, 2011.

3. IBM survey, "Do Multinationals Really Understand Globalization?" *BusinessWeek*, August 2010, www.businessweek.com/globalbiz/content/aug2010/gb2010086_282527.htm#p2.

4. Jeffrey Immelt, Vijay Govindarajan, and Chris Trimble, "How GE Is Disrupting Itself," *Harvard Business Review*, October 2009.

5. "Tom Keene Talks to Harvard's Clay Christensen," Businessweek.com, January 3, 2013.

6. See "Apple's Emerging Market Problem—Seeking Alpha," *Times of India*, October 3, 2012; "Apple Has Ceded the Crown to Samsung in Emerging Markets," *Times of India*, September 22, 2012.

CHAPTER 10

1. Carla Power, "India's Leading Export: CEOs," *Time*, August 1, 2011.

2. "Fighting for the Next Billion Shoppers," *The Economist*, June 30, 2012.

INDEX

ACKNOWLEDGMENTS

If I have seen farther than others, it is only because
I stood on the shoulders of giants.

—SIR ISAAC NEWTON

This book represents the contributions of many thoughtful and generous colleagues and friends.

I am particularly grateful to Anand P. Raman of *Harvard Business Review*, who sharpened my writing with his incisive feedback and was responsible for encouraging me to embark on this project in the first place. Thanks also to the fabulous and highly professional team at Harvard Business Review Press, who were a delight to work with.

My colleagues at Truepoint Partners have been wonderful thought partners throughout this journey. Thank you, Mike Beer, Flemming Norrgren, Nathaniel Foote, Shankar Raman, Malcolm Wolf, and, most of all, Russ Eisenstat.

I owe a particular debt to Alok Kshirsagar, the director of the Asia Center at McKinsey & Company for being generous in sharing ideas, data, and possibilities. I am grateful to Ananth Narayanan of McKinsey and to Karthik Ananth and Pari Natarajan of Zinnov for the discussion on innovation and offshore R&D in India.

I owe a particular debt to Alok Kshirsagar, director of McKinsey & Company and leader of its Asia Center practice, for being generous in sharing ideas, data, and possibilities. I am grateful also to Ananth Narayanan of McKinsey for many thoughtful discussions on innovation and Vimal Choudhary and his team of research specialists for supporting my research.

I am grateful to the Rockefeller Foundation for enabling an extraordinarily productive and agreeable residency at the Bellagio Center.

I am deeply indebted to a large number of thoughtful leaders who willingly shared their ideas, experiences, and time. If the book is rich, it is only thanks to their willingness to share their stories. Among them: the late C. K. Prahalad; professor Bala Chakravarty of IMD, Sir Anthony Bamford, Alan Blake, Vipin Sondhi, Amit Gossain, and John Kavanagh at JCB; Louis Schweitzer, Leif Johansson, and Olof Persson at AB Volvo; Tim Solso and Tom Linebarger at Cummins; D. Shivakumar and Stephen Elop at Nokia; John Flannery at GE; Jean-Pascal Tricoire and Olivier Blum at Schneider Electric; Gabriela Prunier at Suez Environment; Govind Iyer and Claudio Fernández-Aráoz at Egon Zehnder; Craig Mundie at Microsoft; Nitin Paranjpe, Yuri Jain, and Leena Nair at Hindustan Unilever; Shane Tedjarati, Krishna Mikkileni, and Anant Maheshwari at Honeywell; Marc Nassif, S. Nakamura, and Carlos Ghosn at Renault; R. C. Bhargava at Maruti Suzuki; Hans Vestberg and F. Jedjling at Ericsson; S. Vishwanathan at Bosch; Jacques Challes at L'Oréal India; Antonio Helio Waszyk at Nestlé; Scott Price at Walmart; Amit Jatia, Hardcastle Restaurants; Rajeev Bakshi at Metro India; Ganesh Laminarayan at Dell; Neeraj Swaroop and Jaspal Bindra at Standard Chartered Bank; Patrick Rousseau, Veolia India, Ranjit Shahane at Novartis; David Brennan at AstraZeneca; Alberto Weisser at Bunge; Ed Ludwig and Vince Forlenza at BD; Raj Kalathur and Bharat Vedak at Deere; Zubin Irani and Sandy Diehl at UTC; JS Shin at Samsung; Prema and Jyoti Sagar, Meenu Handa, Karthik Ananth, and Pari Natarajan at Zinnov; and

Michael Bekins at Korn Ferry. I am also deeply obliged to innumerable colleagues at Microsoft, Cummins, Infosys, and Volvo, who have all shaped my thinking.

My thanks to Infosys, especially Kris Gopalakrishnan, Sanjay Purohit, and Sunil Jose Gregory for supporting my research with two terrific interns, Shruti Malani and Navoneil Bhattacharya.

Many friends patiently reviewed endless drafts of my manuscript and provided invaluable feedback and encouragement. I am deeply obliged to Will Poole, Ann Fudge, Govind Iyer, Peter Bijur, Hanne de Mora, Jonathan West, and Wayne Brockbank.

I am grateful to the anonymous reviewers for HBR Press, who took the trouble to read a raw manuscript and provide sharp, yet constructive feedback.

For her unflagging encouragement and support at every stage, I owe an incalculable debt to my wife, Sonali Kulkarni. An accomplished CEO herself, she encouraged me to pursue this endeavor, was a willing sounding board day or night, read endless drafts, dispelled my doubts, and provided me the essential fuel that sustained me throughout this journey. Thank you.

ABOUT THE AUTHOR

RAVI VENKATESAN is the former chairman of Microsoft India and Cummins India.

Under Venkatesan's leadership (2004–2011), India became Microsoft's second-largest presence, as well as one of its fastest growing markets. Microsoft India was consistently rated one of the country's most respected companies, most admired brands, and best employers. Venkatesan was instrumental in creating Microsoft India's Project Shiksha, a computer literacy program that has so far trained over 730,000 schoolteachers in India and improved the lives of thirty-five million students. In 2011, Venkatesan was voted India's Most Influential Multinational CEO in the annual survey conducted by the *Economic Times*, the country's leading business newspaper.

Prior to joining Microsoft, Venkatesan worked for sixteen years at Cummins Inc. After serving in several key roles at Cummins in the United States, he moved back to India in 1996. As chairman of Cummins India, he led the company's transformation into India's leading provider of power solutions and largest manufacturer of engines. Venkatesan helped establish the Cummins College of Engineering, India's first engineering college for women, in Pune.

Venkatesan is currently a director on the boards of AB Volvo and Infosys and a fellow of the Center for Higher Ambition Leadership, a nonprofit organization dedicated to developing and supporting a global community of business leaders whose sense of purpose goes beyond achieving financial success for themselves and their institutions. An adviser to several family businesses and entrepreneurial ventures, he is a member of the advisory boards of Bunge Limited and Marico Innovation Foundation, and he serves on Harvard Business School's Global Alumni Board. He is also a founding partner and chairman of Social Venture Partners India, a network of philanthropists addressing complex social issues through venture philanthropy.

Venkatesan holds a bachelor's degree in mechanical engineering from the Indian Institute of Technology, Bombay (1985), a master's degree in industrial engineering from Purdue University (1986), and an MBA from Harvard Business School (1992), where he was a Baker Scholar. Ravi has written two articles for the *Harvard Business Review*. He was awarded the Indian Institute of Technology's Distinguished Alumnus Award in 2003 and Purdue University's Distinguished Engineering Alumnus Award in 2011.

Venkatesan is married to Sonali Kulkarni and lives in Bangalore, India. He can be reached at ravi_venkatesan@hotmail.com.